Classics of American Literature
Part I

Professor Arnold Weinstein

THE TEACHING COMPANY ®

PUBLISHED BY:

THE TEACHING COMPANY
4151 Lafayette Center Drive, Suite 100
Chantilly, Virginia 20151-1232
1-800-TEACH-12
Fax—703-378-3819
www.teach12.com

ISBN 1-56585-811-5

Arnold L. Weinstein, Ph.D.

Edna and Richard Salomon Distinguished Professor
and Professor of Comparative Literature
Brown University

Arnold Weinstein was born in Tennessee in 1940 and received his undergraduate degree in romance languages from Princeton University in 1962. He studied at Université de Paris in 1960–'61 and at Freie Universitat, Berlin, in 1962–'63. He received his master's and doctorate in comparative literature from Harvard University in 1964 and 1968, respectively.

Dr. Weinstein has been teaching courses on European, English, and American literature at Brown University since 1968. In addition, he is the sponsor of Swedish Studies at Brown. He has been the chairperson of the Advisory Council on Comparative Literature at Princeton University and is actively involved in the American Comparative Literature Association.

Among the many academic honors, research grants, and fellowships he has received include research grants from the American Council of Learned Societies and the National Endowment for the Humanities. In 1983, he was visiting professor of American Literature at Stockholm University, where he received the Fulbright Senior Lecturer Award. He is currently a member of the Academy of Literary Studies and the director of a NEH-funded program in great books. In 1995, he was named Brown University's best teacher in the humanities. He is the recipient of a National Endowment for the Humanities Award for University Teachers for 1998–'99 for his work in literature and medicine.

Dr. Weinstein is the author of *Vision and Response in Modern Fiction* (1984), *Fictions of the Self: 1550–1800* (1981), *The Fiction of Relationship* (1988), and *Nobody's Home: Speech, Self, and Place in American Fiction from Hawthorne to DeLillo* (1993). He is working in the fields of literature and medicine, with a view toward a book-length study of the relationship between the two, especially concerning the issues of diagnosis and interpretation.

Table of Contents

Classics of American Literature
Part I

Classics of American Literature

Scope:

We all read many books over our lifetimes, but how many of them do we really remember? We have all heard of the great names in American literature—Emerson, Thoreau, Poe, Hawthorne, Melville, Whitman, Dickinson, Twain, James, Hemingway, Fitzgerald, Faulkner, Eliot, O'Neill, Morrison—but do we know why they are great? Do we truly savor these books in such a way that they are a part of our inner landscape, part of the way we now see America and ourselves?

Of course, many of the books that are considered classics of American literature are part of everyone's repertory. But have we made them into personal knowledge? We know that Rip Van Winkle falls asleep for 20 years for some mysterious reason—but what exactly? Why did Emerson believe in "self-reliance," and why do we? Thoreau went to Walden Pond to force nature into utterance. Is this a victory? An escape? A fiction? Melville's Ahab does war with the white whale. Is his struggle heroic or sacrilegious—mad or impotent? Whitman celebrates the common man, the great city, even life and death. But is he believable? Stowe shows us Uncle Tom, black slave turned into Christ figure—how much has changed since then? Dickinson, the recluse of Amherst, writes the most explosive verse of the century—how could she know what she knew? Twain, our greatest showman, tells a story with an inkling of Peter Pan: Tom Sawyer never does grow up, but Huck Finn must face the racism of the South and somehow get past his own polluted conscience—can he do it? James brings American innocents to Europe for them to inherit the world—but do they?

In the 20th century, Hemingway speaks for a lost generation of American writers who discovered Paris but lost home and self in the bargain. Fitzgerald's Gatsby is the crown prince of capitalism, the hero of self-invention. He finishes up poorly, but Willy Loman, Arthur Miller's salesman-hero, finishes even worse as the American dream turns into a nightmare—have we lost our truest faith? Faulkner's decaying South is alive with ghosts—can there be a future if we are all ghost-ridden? Ellison writes the epic story of an entire race in the adventures of his "invisible man," and Morrison harks all the way back to the horrors of slavery in *Beloved*, joining Stowe, Twain, and Faulkner to remind us, just as the stories of the concentration camps remind us, that even carnage may be survivable—but, at what cost?

American classics are wonderfully rich fare. These books are often the sites of great conflict—political, racial, sexual, and moral. More than any other modern nation, America is a mythic land, a place with a sense of its own destiny and promise, a place that has experienced bloody wars to achieve that destiny. The events of American history shimmer forth in our classics. The Puritan origins and the Revolutionary War have pride of place in much of Hawthorne. The search for an American language—for the great American theme of freedom—is at the core of Emerson, Thoreau, and Whitman. The nightmares of slavery and fratricide, inseparable from the Civil War, inform the vision not only of Stowe, Melville, and Twain, but also of Faulkner and Morrison. America's loss of innocence in World War I, coupled with its enduring belief in the self-made man, reappear as both fact and fiction, as promises that may be unkeepable, in Hemingway, Fitzgerald, T.S. Eliot, and Arthur Miller. Somewhat like a great voyage across the United States, then, especially a voyage in time, we explore our country in these books, an exploration unimaginable in any other form.

Learning Objectives

Upon completion of this course, you should be able to:

1. Explain the role of "self-reliance" and the "self-made man" in the evolution of American literature.

2. Identify the central tenets of American Romanticism.

3. Describe the evolution of the American ghost story, from Poe and Hawthorne to James and Morrison.

4. Outline the epic strain in American literature, from Melville and Whitman to Faulkner and Ellison.

5. Explain the importance of slavery as a critical subject matter for Stowe, Twain, Faulkner, and Morrison.

6. Summarize the perspective on nature revealed in such seminal poets as Whitman, Dickinson, Frost, and Eliot.

7. Identify the main tenets of Modernism in the work of Eliot, Fitzgerald, Hemingway, and Faulkner.

8. Identify the major contributions of O'Neill, Miller, and Williams to American theater.

9. Summarize the major threads of the complex relationship between America's great writers and the past.

Lecture One
Introduction to *Classics of American Literature*

Scope:

A course on American classics should begin with some sense of what a "classic" is, what is "American" about this project, and what one can expect from this endeavor. "Classic" is the great honorific term that often implies staleness: we rarely expect our classics to be shocking or exciting or disturbing. All too often, we approach them with piety and boredom, seeing in them the enshrined monuments to crusty traditions. Classics are indeed those canonical texts of American literature that many of us have grown up with, but they are neither innocuous nor asleep; on the contrary, they have the power to unhinge us. They stem out of vital, often unresolvable conflicts from their own moment. They are bristling with ambiguities and insights that bid to challenge or destabilize us, even today. Even tomorrow. Our approach here is to discover the rich multidimensional manna that rests within these works, waiting to be revealed. Moreover, we will consider the names on this august list with a sense of what is timely as well as timeless. The canon changes, and many of our most revered writers today were unheard-of a while back and may be eclipsed again in the years to come, while others whom we have never read will step in to fill those shoes. Finally, these literary masterpieces can be thought of as bottles with a special genie within them. Our objective is to open the bottle and free a number of miracles: the actuality of the past, the great American story that begins for us with Benjamin Franklin and goes on to Toni Morrison; and the shimmering world of feelings and imagination, of desire and fear, that is not recorded in history but that art captures and keeps alive for us centuries later, giving us a script that is radically different from anything else we have. Accessing the great American books, the classics, is a unique way of understanding the history of this country and of adding to our own personal estate of literary wealth.

Objectives: Upon completion of this lecture, you should be able to:

1. Explain the pitfalls inherent in the very notion of a "classic."

2. Summarize the unique role of literature in revealing human experience.

3. Explain the appropriateness of the "journey" metaphor in revisiting American literature.

Outline

I. It is useful to begin a course on the Classics of American Literature by asking some central questions about these terms.

    A. What do we mean by "classic"?

        1. Mark Twain expresses the most widespread, if unacknowledged, view of all: a classic is a book that nobody reads.

        2. Ezra Pound, pioneering spirit of literary Modernism, claimed that classics have a special freshness about them that never stales.

        3. Harold Bloom, eminent American critic, has argued that the key feature of our canonical books is their uncompromising strangeness. Not only are they strange, but also they make the world a stranger place.

    B. What do we take to be the American classics? For the most part, this course accepts the configuration of the canon as it now stands.

        1. We will read key texts from key authors over the past 250 years: Benjamin Franklin, Washington Irving, Ralph Waldo Emerson, Henry David Thoreau, Edgar Allan Poe, Nathaniel Hawthorne, Herman Melville, Walt Whitman, Harriet Beecher Stowe, Emily Dickinson, Mark Twain, Henry James, Stephen Crane, Charlotte Perkins Gilman, Robert Frost, T.S. Eliot, F. Scott Fitzgerald, Ernest Hemingway, William Faulkner, John Steinbeck, Ralph Ellison, Eugene O'Neill, Tennessee Williams, Arthur Miller, and Toni Morrison.

        2. There are some notable omissions in this list. James Fenimore Cooper, Kate Chopin, Willa Cather, Theodore Dreiser, Richard Wright, and a host of significant modern writers such as Saul Bellow and Thomas Pynchon, will not be covered. Would that they could be. *Mea culpa.*

        3. But the list also has its surprises. Gilman is not a name that everyone knows, yet her astonishing story of the 1890s, "The Yellow Wall-Paper," is indisputably a classic today, as is evidenced by its inclusion in courses

on American literature and women's literature throughout the country. We also will review unknown texts by famous authors that deserve wider recognition: hence, included as potent, stunning surprises on this list are Hawthorne's tale "Wakefield," Melville's story "Benito Cereno," Twain's novel *Pudd'nhead Wilson,* and Hemingway's posthumous novel *The Garden of Eden.* These works will challenge many of the views we have of these established authors.

4. Even though this final list may appear engraved in stone, such appearances are deeply misleading. Just as Galileo said of the earth, one must also say of the canon: "Nonetheless, it moves." The great texts in literature are "determined" to be great by writers, scholars, critics, readers, and publishers. Thoreau was not taken truly seriously until our century; Melville and Dickinson were virtually unheard-of in their own time; Faulkner was out of print until the mid-'40s; and Fitzgerald died thinking he had been forgotten and some of those who are included—Steinbeck, and conceivably Eliot and Hemingway—would be stridently rejected by many literary scholars today. Writers' reputations rise and fall, like valuations on the stock market. A few, like Shakespeare, seem to have something for every age, every taste. Others can appear unreadable or silly or dreadfully compromised at a later date. Still others whom we have ignored will find their places after we are dead.

5. There are to be no pieties in this course, except for one: the willingness to take these figures seriously. But we will not place them on pedestals, and we will be prepared to ask them hard questions, questions having to do with our agendas as much as theirs. We must be prepared, however, for the hard questions they will also ask of us.

II. Literature exists as a window into a culture—these texts, seen together, tell us about America.

   A. Literature offers us a unique form of history, utterly unlike the discipline of history itself.

1. We will place little emphasis on dates or "facts" in the sense of information to be memorized or on "schools" whose features and rules need to be memorized.

2. The great virtue of literature (of art in general) is that it does not truck with abstract data, such as the dates of battles or elections, the numbers of this or that, or the rules or laws of this or that. One could argue that such "data" are rarely real for us, in any experiential sense, and that the business of art is precisely to translate data and information into living circumstance, to turn fact into fiction. It may seem that such a procedure moves away from reality, but the opposite is true. Facts start to live when we see them as part of experience, even fictive experience.

3. Hence, this course offers a vision of America. It is the *storied* past of this country—its geographic regions, its explorations overseas, its historical past (going back to the Puritans), and its resonance of still earlier stories from antiquity that helped shape the writer's views.

4. Some of these portraits of America are very focused, such as Thoreau's stint at Walden Pond, Whitman's crossing by Brooklyn Ferry, Frost's New Hampshire, and Faulkner's "Yoknapatawpha." Others are sweeping and global—Melville's tales of adventure and misadventure at sea, Eliot's sense of the entire European tradition, Hemingway's discovery (for him and for us) of Paris and Pamplona, and Steinbeck's pilgrimage of Okies on the road.

B. Literature packages information in a special form: that of stories. What does this mean?

1. Events come to us in the shape of human lives. Events appear to us as the dynamics of living people (rather than as data in books for students to memorize). The Salem Witch Trials, the Revolutionary War, the Civil War, the Gold Rush, the lure of Europe, the Great War of 1914–'18, the giddy '20s and the dreary '30s all appear in their impact on lives, as human experience.

2. Hence, art tells us about human experience, human feelings, in a way that no other discipline approaches. Art revels in subjectivity. And it poses the question: What do we actually know about the feelings of others? What do history and census books and even photographs and maps teach us about the "inner" world?

3. Who could write your life? What could even the savviest historian know about you? This is the kind of knowledge and information that art possesses. It is a story we would not otherwise have.

4. Thus, these books give us an inside story of America. Irving and Hawthorne speak to us about the disruption of the Revolutionary War, as America became America—instead of remaining an English colony. Melville and Stowe wrote about slavery before the Civil War, and we can see it coming; Twain and Faulkner and Morrison show us, years after actual events occurred, even a century later, that the issues of race and slavery embodied in that war are still with us today. The collapse of values heralded by World War I, and sealed by the Great Depression, come to us in vivid form in Eliot, Fitzgerald, Hemingway, and Steinbeck.

5. Not only do these authors speak in their moment, but many of them show us that the still earlier, more remote past lives on, often insidiously, in its favorite form: inside of human beings. Hawthorne, writing in bustling Jacksonian mid-19th-century America, is haunted by the Puritan past; Faulkner and Morrison are virtually inhabited by older stories that must still be told, must somehow be transformed into knowledge. All this goes squarely against our (naive) cult of the future, so much so that our first great ghost writer, Edgar Allan Poe, appears prophetic to us with his insistent fable of "burying people alive." People being buried alive is a perfect formula for the living past, indeed for human memory itself.

C. Not only does literature present its information as story, but it also offers us privileged access to its materials.

1. The art of the past contains the living blood of the past. Reading can be compared to vampirism, to blood transfusions, or to old wines whose living grapes of 20 or even 50 years ago still have fire when we open the bottle.

2. Whitman's title for one of his poems, "Song of the Open Road," can symbolize the journey that literature has always offered readers. This voyage from book to life, from now to then, here to there, me to you, is often imaged in unforgettable ways in these texts: Whitman who waits for you on the ferry, or on the path; Faulkner's college roommates who "enter" into the Civil War a half century after the fact; and Morrison's living ghost, who reestablishes the broken circulation system of the novel, adumbrates that mysterious mother tongue that unites mothers and daughters over time, leading back to Africa itself and the first slave ships.

3. These images of voyage and continuity radically challenge our customary sense of living here-and-now, living as someone with finite contours. These texts invite us to extend our own boundaries, to process something of the collective wealth of America.

4. And, because they are the classics that many of us read long ago, but perhaps never quite turned into personal knowledge, never quite knew why they were classics, these books invite us to make good on our own pasts, to reclaim our own estate. We will experience the magic joy of storytelling.

5. My role is guide. I bring with me my particular background and biases. I emphasize the great American theme of freedom and self-making and explore how difficult such a thing is. In reading the classics, we are recovering history and transforming it into present experience.

Lecture One—Transcript
Introduction to *Classics of American Literature*

Let me welcome you to this course on classic texts in American literature. This is obviously going to be the introduction, and in this lecture I intend to sketch out the parameters of the course, talk as well about the rationale of the course and give you some sense of what you're in for. It sort of sounds like a jail sentence. These are texts that are thought of as the monuments of American literature. "The Classics" is a kind of dicey term. It works against you, as well as for you. There are lots of definitions of classics. The one that I think is the most on-the-money is Twain's definition, that "a classic is a book that nobody reads," by which I think he means to say that it's a book that is enshrined; it's on a pedestal; it's usually dusty, and it's crusty, too. It's thought to be a kind of pious statement of the received values of a particular period, which makes it somewhat dull and conservative. People usually read classics when they're required to—in a course or something like that.

I want to read a couple of alternative definitions that are closer to what I have in mind. Here's one that Ezra Pound gave: "A classic is classic not because it conforms to certain structural rules or fits certain definitions of which its author had quite probably never heard. It is classic because of a certain eternal and irrepressible freshness." It's just the opposite of dusty, crusty. It's fresh. I also want to site Harold Bloom, who is a very distinguished critic at Yale. He's talking about canonical texts—and it could be the classics as well—he says that, when you read a canonical work for the first time, "you encounter a stranger, an uncanny startlement, rather than a fulfillment of expectations." I like Bloom's emphasis there because, even though he's talking about Western literature in general, and the great canonical texts, I think it works also for our list of American texts in this course. They are texts that are startling, that are strange, that are the opposite of what we expect, that have surprises for us, that are unpredictable, and also unlike one another.

This is not going to be a kind of confirmation of some already fairly well known notion of American literature. At least I hope it won't be that. I want it to shock us, to surprise us. I want you to realize as well—or to agree with me at least in part—that these texts can be very unsettling, that they can be destabilizing, that they are themselves often unresolved, that it's not easy to get a bottom line reading on the books that we're going to read. What are the books we're going to read? They are the usual suspects. I'll list them for you: Franklin, Irving, Emerson, Thoreau, Poe, Hawthorne, Melville, Whitman, Stowe, Dickinson, Twain, James, Crane, Gilman, Frost, Eliot, Fitzgerald, Hemingway, Faulkner, Steinbeck, Ellison, O'Neill, Williams, Miller, Morrison. As I say, the usual suspects.

Those of you who've done a lot of work in American literature will recognize that there are some omissions, and I want to acknowledge that up front. Cooper is not in this course, and he really deserves a place there. The *Leatherstocking Tales* are part of American mythology. Likewise, Kate Chopin, who is one of the great, discovered authors of the late 19th century, is not there—but Gilman is going to sort of be her substitute. Willa Cather's not there. Edith Wharton's not there. Dreiser's not there. Dos Passos is not there. Richard Wright's not there. Among contemporary figures, the only contemporary author that I'm putting in the course is Toni Morrison. So Saul Bellow and Thomas Pynchon are not there, and other authors that I've dealt with in other courses for The Teaching Company, like Vonnegut, Coover, or DeLillo. They do not find their place in this course.

There are some surprises. As I mentioned, Charlotte Perkins Gilman is a name that not everyone recognizes, and yet, she is a classic. Her story, "The Yellow Wall-Paper," is now part of the canon in American literature—and I hope it's an exciting surprise for you. And then I've included some texts by well-known authors, but the texts themselves are not well known. So I'm going to give a whole lecture on Hawthorne's "Wakefield," which I think is one of the most uncanny pieces written in the 19th century and looks like it's a 20th century text. It looks like it is "Kafka" already. I'm going to give two lecturers on Melville's astonishing story, "Benito Cereno," because I think it's a story that is not only one of the most telling documents we have about the status of racism in the mid-19th century—before the Civil War—about the status of blacks, but it's also a prescient text. It's a text that looks towards, I think—misadventures of American foreign policy—but it's about Americans in the dark in the high seas, not knowing about the cultures that they pretend or think they understand. I also think it looks to some of our wars.

Then I'm going to include a very under-read but wonderful book by Mark Twain after looking at texts like *Tom Sawyer* and particularly *Huckleberry Finn*. I'm going to include *Pudd'nhead Wilson*, which partly is a book that intrigues me because I'm a twin. It's a book about twins, but it's a book also about the mix of black and white that Twain is still wrestling with many years after the Civil War. Then the other surprise text—the other sort of sleeper, as it were—is Hemingway's posthumous text, *The Garden of Eden*, which I'm going to include in my discussion of Hemingway—two lectures on it—after a couple of lectures on *The Sun Also Rises*. *The Garden of Eden* is really a kind of sexual fantasia. It's a kind of text in which a lot of the Hemingway phantoms and a lot of the Hemingway skeletons become visible to us and come out of the closet.

I said the usual suspects, and this list may appear to you to be fixed in stone. Yet, the canon is always moving. It's like Galileo described the earth, "Nonetheless it moves," he said. And despite the views of the Church, that the earth is the center point of the universe and the sun goes around it, the earth moves. The canon moves as well. It's not easy for us to always remember that. These are names that most of us assume have always been important in American literature. Well, that's not true. Thoreau was not taken seriously until our century, even though people in the 19th century knew who he was. Melville and Dickinson, people didn't know who they were, particularly Dickinson. They were virtually unheard of in their time. It's only in this century that they have achieved canonical status. Faulkner was out of print until the mid-1940s, even though he got the Nobel Prize in 1950. He'd already written all of his greatest books by then. Fitzgerald died in 1940 thinking that he was a forgotten writer and that no one would attend to his work. Some of the choices that I have included, such as Steinbeck or Eliot—or conceivably even Hemingway—would be fiercely debated or disputed by critics, particularly younger critics, today. The stock of writers is like the stock market. It goes up, it goes down, it rises, and it falls. Reputations rise and fall. Some writers, like Shakespeare, offer something for every age. They're reconstructed and remade, generation after generation. Other writers become unreadable to us or become silly or become very compromised. Still other writers, whom we have never heard of, are going to be unearthed in 10, 20, or 30 years, and it will be said to the readers in 30 years, "they speak for us." Yet, we don't know who they are. The canon changes.

I'm going to try to avoid pieties in the course. As I said, this is not a course about genuflecting in front of the grand works of the tradition. There is one piety that I will insist on, and that is that one take the work seriously—to put it more simply, that you read the books. That, in itself, is not easy to do. It's hard to read some of these books. We've got some very difficult as well as some very delightful kinds of texts in it. We will want to ask hard questions of these books, questions that have to do with our values and our assumptions, because those are the questions we always ask. We cannot, in fact, free ourselves of our own moment. For authors, for example, that did not have race or gender primarily in mind; we're going to ask those questions because they matter to us. The converse is also true. These books will ask us hard questions that are not our questions but theirs. It's worthwhile for us to be willing to stretch and reach and understand what questions they're posing, the challenges that they present to us, and our way of doing business.

The course is, in some sense, a kind of search for America. I want to argue here that, in reading this spectrum of books from Benjamin Franklin to Toni Morrison, we're going to get a very special kind of excursion into American history. It's literature—and not history—and I can't emphasize that enough. I'm going to be talking about it a lot in the remainder of this lecture. There's going to be virtually no emphasis on dates, even though the dates will be mentioned in the outlines. There's going to be virtually no emphasis on facts. I'm not sure that facts mean much in art. I'm not going to emphasize literary schools. I'm not going to emphasize particular tenets or rules of this school or that school, even though I will, in fact, allude to realism, naturalism, symbolism, impressionism, and expressionism. That's not the purpose of the course, to quantify these rules and then to feel like we have it nailed down. My own view—and this is very personal because you may not agree with this—is that one's eyes glaze over at the sight of dates and of facts. That's why I was always a very poor student of history. It didn't make sense to me. It was never real. It was something you could easily memorize and spit back on an exam; but it rarely had much resonance to it.

It's important, it seems to me, to transform the data that we have—and the data that we have from the past is often very slight and slim—into something that is real for us, into something that is experiential for us. That's what I think literature does. It translates data and information, which we have so much of in our age. We are the great information age, but we're short on experience. Art translates information into experience. It turns facts, if you will, into fictions. Although our immediate notion is that, when we're dealing with fictions, we're at several removes from reality, the opposite is the truth. It's only when facts become fictions, when they become stories, when they become experiential—even if it's the experience of characters—that's the only time they become real. That's when we realize what they're all about in the first place. These texts bear witness to an American experience. In fact, they suggest a view of America "as" experience. Therefore, I think this course represents a kind of composite experiential take on some 250 years of history, but it is a "storied" take—it's packaged in the form of stories. I hope that there is ample spread here. We're going to read about stories of the entire nation, of east and west, north and south, men and women. Children will be prominent in some of these texts, as well New England, California, and the open seas. The temporal spread is just as great, if not greater, than the spatial spread. It is a past that goes easily back to the Puritan heritage with which this country began, to the Native Americans as well who will find their way into some of the texts of Hawthorne. There are also fables that go further back than the founding of America, fables that go back to our oldest stories, such as the *The Garden of Eden* which is the title of Hemingway's text, or biblical stories such as the House of David, which is going to be central in one of Faulkner's books.

Some of these texts are going to be very, very focused about a particular place at a particular time. For instance, there is Thoreau's stint in Walden Pond in the middle of the 19th century, Whitman's "Crossing Brooklyn Ferry" also in the very mid years of the 19th century, Frost's sense of New Hampshire in the early years of this century, Faulkner's "Yoknapatawpha," that postage stamp of soil—Mississippi in the 1920s and 1930s. Sometimes the vantage point will be much broader, more global. For instance, there are Melville's tales of adventure and also of misadventure at sea, Eliot's evocation of the entire European tradition and beyond Europe in "The Waste Land," Hemingway's pilgrimage to Paris, and in a sense, a whole generation of readers, who saw Paris through Hemingway's eyes, but also to Pamplona and to Africa. There is Steinbeck's pilgrimage of a very different sort, of Okies on the road, crossing the United States, moving to what they thought of as the Garden of Eden—California—which turns out to be a great, great tragic disappointment. I repeat, literature, not history. Stories, not information, not abstract data, not laws, not facts, not events, but the shape of human lives, which is to say the impact of events—of grand events. What do we think the real meaning would be of the Salem witch trials, or of the Revolutionary War, or of the California Gold Rush, or of the American Civil War, or of the discovery of Europe in the early '20s and '30s, the lure of Paris, the disenchantment that comes in with the great war, World War I, the giddy '20s, the flappers, or the Depression?

We can memorize a number of facts about these key moments in American history, but what we're going to find here is how these moments impact on human lives, how these moments become visible to us as an experiential reality. I want to suggest that, in some sense, is what the meaning of these events is as they are translated into the fabric of life, not simply something that we can see in a history book—the fabric of life, the experience of people. In saying that, I want to emphasize, that is, of course, what we never know about other people or about the past. What record do we have of people's experiences? We have a lot of other records. We have records of the things that we can measure. We have records of the things that people can paint. We have modern records of the things that can be photographed. But all of this quantification is essentially locked out of the inner worlds that are central to art—imagination, feeling, libido, desire—all of that which is what literature trucks in, revels in. All of that is not available to our empirical sciences, and even, I think, to history.

Let me go further. What do we ever know about the feelings of people in general? No one ever presents himself or herself to us with their heart on their sleeves or with their past written on their foreheads. We are in the dark as to what people are really like on the inside. Literature offers us a version of that. It certainly can't be a kind of true version, a provable version—a testable version. Nonetheless, it offers us a version of that. Of that huge world on the inside, "the place where the meanings are" is the way Dickinson describes it. The place, in fact, where the outside events ultimately end up. How do we learn about that? Think about it personally. Who could write your story? What historian would ever know enough to write your life? You know the huge discrepancy between the few, recorded events of your life, what you put on a CV or a resume, and the huge swollen interior record that is otherwise in the dark. Art opens up that record.

These texts are going to write that for us. It's soft, if you think in terms of data and facts, but it's a record that we wouldn't otherwise have—those events that I refer to, shimmer in this course. About 1820, Washington Irving writes a story of a man who falls asleep during the Revolutionary War. That's exactly the period through which he sleeps. In the 1830s, Hawthorne writes a story called "My Kinsman, Major Molineux" about a young man who goes to Boston on the eve of the revolution. It's a city that is unreadable, that's jumping out of its skin, because it's about a country that's jumping out of its skin, that is on the verge of no longer being a British colony but becoming what we think of as America. We see these things. We see the vitality, the becoming of these things, in these texts.

Our own great national founding trauma, the Civil War, shimmers through texts written before it. We see it in Stowe's *Uncle Tom's Cabin*. We see the discourse on slavery. We see it even more acutely, in Melville's "Benito Cereno." We also see it after 1865. We see its continuing legacy and unresolved tensions in Twain's *Huckleberry Finn* and *Pudd'nhead Wilson*, written in the 1880s and 1890s, where Twain goes back, revisits the south, revisits the issues of black and white. And it won't go away. We see it again in 1936 when Faulkner writes *Absolom! Absolom!*. We see it further anguished in Morrison's *Beloved* of 1988. One hundred and twenty years after the war, and it's still playing, still being revisited, still being unpacked, still being processed into some kind of knowledge. There is also the trauma and shattered world of World War II. It produces that "Waste Land" culture that Eliot chronicles for us, or it produces the frenetic antics of figures like Jake Barnes and his friends in Hemingway's *The Sun Also Rises*. Our history is palpable in these books, whether it's the Okies on the road in the 1930s, whether it's Manhattan as Whitman walked it and talked it in 1850, whether it's Philadelphia that young Ben Franklin is walking down the streets of, munching bread in the 1720s. All of that lives in these kinds of texts. Writers deliver their moment.

That's not all. Many of them show us that other, still earlier moments are still alive. They're haunted. Hawthorne is writing in mid-19th century—bustling Jacksonian America. What does he do? He goes back 200 years to write about his ancestors in those Salem witch trials, to write about a strange mysterious woman with a red "A" emblem—and what does it mean? Faulkner and Morrison are even further haunted about a war that took place from 1861 to 1865. They feel their way into this quagmire, the fratricidal passions in Faulkner and the crippling legacy of slavery in Morrison.

Our creator of ghost stories, Edgar Allan Poe, tells over and over the same story, about burying people alive, from Madeline Usher to Fortunato in "The Cask of Amontillado," here bodies that are walled off but that keep on living, reappearing like they do in his story "The Black Cat." I want you to think about that image, burying people alive. What a perfect image of history that is. That is the past. The dead are not dead. They're alive. We think they're buried away and quiet, but that's not the case. It's an image of the living past, dead people who aren't dead, people who still speak, whose voices we have to hear. That's not all. It's an image of human memory. It's what our own psyche is like, all of the people within us who are not cadavers, who are still voices, our own past, the past of others that still lives. Literature makes room for them and makes those voices visible.

Through literature we recover this kind of rich, bristling material. We access it. It's a little bit vampire-ish at times—it sounds like a little bit of a blood transfusion. I would compare it, in a more congenial metaphor, to wines—old wines. We open an old wine, and particularly a wine that may be 20, 30, or 40 years old—I've actually drunk wines that are over 40 years old, and I drank them, and they're wines that come from that 18th century that can still be drunk. When you open that bottle—if you still have a cork that hasn't come apart—the grapes that were harvested 10, 20, 50 years ago, 100 years ago, the people who harvested them who are now dead, all of that lives in the wine. You taste it, and it's this kind of magic sort of embodiment, magic ingesting of the past. Whitman, in one of his great poems, used the phrase, "the song of the open road." That's what literature is; books are an open road, a route into other lives.

These writers are not just our itinerary, but they're their waiting for us. Here's how Whitman closes "Song of Myself."

> I depart as air, I shake my white locks at the runaway sun,
>
> I effuse my flesh in eddies, and drift it in lacy jags.

> I bequeath myself to the dirt to grow from the grass I love,

> If you want me again look for me under your boot-soles.

Where is Whitman? He's saying, not on the page, not in the library, not in this course, he's under your boot soles. You encounter Whitman every time you walk. He has an uncanny sense of our encounter with him being the purpose of art. "Crossing Brooklyn Ferry" centralizes the notion of the ferry ride itself, which is clearly an emblem of reading, of entering into the waterway of art, literature, history, and time. He is there as our guide.

> Closer yet I approach you,

> What thought you have of me now, I had as much of you -

> I laid in my stores in advance,

> I considered long and seriously of you before you were born.

> Who was to know what should come home to me?

> Who knows but I am enjoying this?

This is the man writing. He's been dead so long now, and yet every time we read that line, we have this ghostly presence that got there before we did, who crafted this strategic encounter between us and them, which is the reading of the text, "Who knows for all the distance but I am as good as looking at you now, for all you cannot see me? "

Faulkner will take the same notion and make a beautiful emblem of it in *Absolom! Absolom!,* where you have two young boys, college roommates, one from Canada, one from Mississippi, in a Harvard dormitory, trying to make sense of something that happened 50 years earlier, in 1861, when two other boys, who were their counterparts, left this Mississippi plantation. We have this beautiful image of the two college boys at Cambridge, Massachusetts, becoming the two boys in Mississippi. Faulkner writes, "four boys on two horses" as they then ride across the Mississippi in 1861. That is a perfect emblem again of the voyage, of the itinerary, of the continuity between the past and us.

We're going to see that sense of continuity, of connection, over and over in a text that's one of the most beautiful texts of the course, Ellison's *Invisible Man*, which we might read as a text that is simply a text about a black man. It's about a kind of experience that white readers can't have. Ellison wonderfully closes that book with this line, "Who knows but that on the lower frequencies I speak for you?" And it's an image that's a kind of modern image—the lower frequencies—it's a kind of electronic wavelength image. It states the universality of his text. That's a dirty word in today's culture, "universality." He is writing about a black man's experience. Yet he himself emphasizes, "I am speaking for you." He knew that he had readers who were going to be yellow, white, and red, as well as black. Perhaps the most graphic image of the fluidity of art—the way in which it essentially opens us up into other worlds—comes in Morrison's book *Beloved,* in which the dead return, and they seem to be speaking a never-forgotten language, literally a mother tongue that takes us—as well as the text—back to Africa, back to the slave ships that first brought the slaves over. This text is written virtually in liquids, the liquids of the body—blood, water, urine, milk— showing a kind of core fluidity, like the blood in Faulkner, a kind of navigational waterway that connects us to others, to the past, and to art.

These are all images of voyage and continuity. What they all do is they make you redefine who you are and where you are. We have a lazy, small-minded notion that we are here and now, that our lives stop at the edges of our own bodies, that our lives are essentially confined by the dates of our birth and death. Of course art tells us— as experience does all the time—that that's not true. We can live in the past. We can live in the "might have been." We can live life in the future. We can live in dreams, desires, and other kinds of narrative scenarios. We can extend our whereabouts, in time and in space, vicariously through art. That's a way of opening and extending and expanding our estate. Of course, that's what a journey through American classical texts is about. It's about that "repossessing" of an estate. I want to emphasize that. In a sense, the technology of this very program puts me into people's living rooms. It establishes a kind of continuity that we can't know in the flesh—I can be present. These texts can be present in places where the authors and perhaps the speaker are dead. That is perfectly parallel with the kind of remarkable extensions and projections and voyages that I've just been talking about.

These books have to constitute a kind of an estate, for most literate Americans. Most of us, in fact, have read these books. If we haven't read them, we've heard of them or we've known about them. I think one of the interesting purposes of this course— I hope it works this way—is that it is a kind of opportunity for a second go around for many of us, and for many of these books, to get a second look at them, a second encounter. Instead of being told they are the classics—they're great—to give us an opportunity to find out why they're classics, why they're great. To see how "strange and fresh" they are, as Pound and Bloom said. It is a chance to return and in that kind of return which is often, in some sense, a return to books that we have read 10, 20, 30, 40 years ago. That too is a kind of expansion of our estate. It's making good on an earlier investment of our self. It's bringing material from the dark, back into the light. That's a really empirical way of looking at it. It's a kind of utilitarian way. I'm saying that I'm going to convert this. These texts are going to be converted into something that is meaningful and valuable to you. I think these texts are something of the collective self-conscious of this country. These texts hum slightly underneath our hearing. We sense that they're valuable. We sense that they might be magic. I hope this is an opportunity for us to make that discovery and make that trip.

I use the word "magic" intentionally. I want, in my lectures on these books, to try to recover something of their magic. Not to treat them as documents only, but to have us all experience the joy of storytelling itself—just the stories, the sight of hypnotic stories themselves—to see that, as well as to try to unpack their meanings. I'm the guide for this for you, with all of my biases. I'm visibly white and male. I come from the south. I have my own views. You will see them for what they are. I am drawn to certain themes. You'll see them for what they are. That is a condition of the course. But, the books that I have said are drenched in history are also being remade right now, as you read them. They are today's books, not just the books of the past.

Lecture Two
Benjamin Franklin's *Autobiography*—
The First American Story

Scope:

Franklin is the towering figure of 18th-century America, but his status as icon is best measured by comparing him, the pragmatic journalist-diplomat-scientist, to his counterpart, Jonathan Edwards, the great theologian philosopher of the same period—Franklin the Yankee vs. Edwards the Puritan. Franklin's career is stunning, spread equally over the fields of science, diplomacy, and unparalleled public service. When he returned to Philadelphia from Paris in 1785, after conducting the political affairs and negotiations with both the English and the French during the crisis of the Revolutionary War as a mere yeoman, he was the most famous private citizen in the Western world. Only a portion of his life experiences are recorded in his *Autobiography*, a work he began in his sixties, but this piece of writing is nonetheless an indubitable American classic—it leaves for posterity the record of a paradigmatic American existence, from modest origins to world celebrity. Franklin's account of his life is larded with wit and moral precepts, and this brand of secular wisdom has not always been to everyone's taste, as we shall see. Like him or not, we have him at the head of the American pantheon, an instance of human self-making of such potency that it quickly becomes what we now know as The American Dream.

Objectives: Upon completion of this lecture, you should be able to:

1. Compare and contrast Franklin's philosophy with that of the Puritan fathers.

2. Summarize the ethos of Franklin and explain how it is typically "American."

3. Outline D.H. Lawrence's major criticisms of Franklin.

Outline

I. Benjamin Franklin appears to us today as the American giant of the 18th century, even though he thought of himself as a British subject until 1776. If we compare Franklin to his exact contemporary, Jonathan Edwards, we can better gauge his significance.

    A. Edwards is the last great Puritan: theologian, intellectual, and author of fierce sermons such as *Sinners in the Hands of an Angry God*. Franklin, by contrast, is a secular figure: printer/scientist/diplomat/ moralist.

        1. The traditional view is that Edwards looked to the past, whereas Franklin pointed to America's future.

        2. Yet, Franklin has had his own sharp critics. Thinkers of many varieties (e.g., Balzac, D.H. Lawrence, and William Carlos Williams) have thought his brand of optimistic secularism to be shallow.

    B. Franklin's astounding list of achievements during his lifetime constitutes a record that no other American, before or since, can match.

        1. His early years consisted of establishing himself as printer, then journalist and writer. From 1732 to 1757 he wrote *Poor Richard's Almanac*, the first American periodical and source of proverbs that is still a bestseller even today.

        2. Franklin's accomplishments in civic and public life are even more striking. A few of his noteworthy contributions include the following: He organized the Union Fire Co. in 1736, became Philadelphia's Postmaster in 1737, proposed the idea for the American Philosophical Society in 1743, organized the Pennsylvania Militia in 1747, and founded the Philadelphia Academy in 1749 (which later became the University of Pennsylvania).

        3. Franklin's exploits in science and technology are equally historic. They include his invention of the Franklin fireplace (stove) in 1741, experiments in electricity in 1745, his assistance in founding Philadelphia Hospital in 1751, and his famous experiment proving that lightning is electricity in 1752.

4. Hostilities between the colonies and England engaged Franklin from the 1760s through the 1780s, as a representative of Pennsylvania, initially, and, after 1776, as chief negotiator of both the war and the peace. Franklin signed both the Declaration of Independence and the Constitution.

5. He worked to abolish slavery, to extend the vote, and to implement a bicameral legislature. He died in 1790.

II. Franklin appears to us, in his writings, as a congenial, albeit shrewd man, one possessed of humor and common sense, both in large doses.

A. *Poor Richard's Almanac*, which Franklin published for 25 years, contains bits of folk wisdom that are still with us today. Moreover, the *Autobiography* reveals a man who was able to laugh at himself even while pontificating. This genial manner characterized Franklin right into his old age, even in elegant Parisian society in the 1780s.

B. *Autobiography* is properly regarded as Franklin's most significant literary achievement, not so much for its own artfulness (though it is artful) as for its status as a great American model of selfhood.

1. Franklin tells the story of his life with certain modesty, but future generations have seen in it the great American rags-to-riches story. From obscure origins in Boston in the 1720s to celebrated man of the world, Franklin moved in a trajectory that helped define American thinking.

2. Franklin reveals himself, in *Autobiography,* to be a profoundly *public* figure, and critics looking for intimate confessions and secrets are disappointed. In this way, he is the counter-model to Rousseau, whose contemporary *Confessions* are a key Romantic document. But Franklin, with or without an "unconscious" on show, makes us understand that the public man and private man were inseparable in 18th-century life. Plus, he provides us with actual strategies for succeeding as a "public" figure, and nowhere is his legacy stronger than in this regard.

3. Franklin also emerged as one of the great 18th-century moralists in that he incessantly preached a kind of

prudent secular wisdom. In some of his most famous pages, these injunctions and "commandments" are rendered in graphic form. He enumerated the 13 key virtues; he kept a weekly scorecard; he devised a scheme for measuring personal development and compliance; and he articulated a universal religious creed.

4. Many subsequent writers have responded sharply to Franklin's "program," but none so savagely and humorously as D.H. Lawrence. Lawrence's critique is useful for perceiving the questionable aspects of the Franklin legacy.

5. Despite all criticisms, however, Franklin remains the enduring American icon of the 18th century, matched only by George Washington. He is with us in countless ways, as emblem of prudent business investments, as subject of countless portraits, and as an often-quoted statesman and inventor. He ultimately demonstrates more perspective than we think: he excelled in grasping others' vantage points and ways of thinking, he knew how to camouflage his own ego, and he was one of our first abolitionists in the slavery debate. Franklin founded the religion of the self-made man, and with it, the American dream.

Readings:

Essential: Franklin, *Autobiography* in *Writings* (Library of America, 1987)

Recommended: Franklin, *Poor Richard's Almanac* in *Writings* (Library of America, 1987); Lawrence, *Studies in Classic American Literature* (Viking, 1964); Barbour, ed. *Benjamin Franklin: Critical Views* (Prentice Hall, 1979)

Topics for Further Consideration:

1. Explain to what extent you think "self-made man" applies to the life and career of Benjamin Franklin.

2. Defend Franklin against the criticisms leveled at him by D.H. Lawrence.

Lecture Two—Transcript
Benjamin Franklin's Autobiography—
The First American Story

This is Lecture Two, and I'm going to speak to you today about one of the giants of American history, Benjamin Franklin. I said history, because it's not really clear that we should consider him as a literary person. His achievements in the field of American Politics are just unbelievable. I intend to enumerate a bunch of them. He did leave us a text called *Autobiography*, however, which I think is fairly seen as one of the seminal texts in American thinking. It's the great story of the self-made man. In that light, he really is the starting point for American literature as well.

In this lecture, I'm going to begin by placing him in a contrastive position with his absolute contemporary, Jonathan Edwards, the Puritan theologian. I'm going to talk about that as a way of trying to spell out or focus on what is interesting and new about Franklin. Then, I think, one is obliged to go through the list of at least a selective number of his achievements and accomplishments, and the kinds of things he did. Most of this lecture is going to be really about *Autobiography* and about his writing. I start with Edwards, however, because he is the great Puritan theologian of the 18th century and of America. He is a brilliant man, a very keen intellect, a kind of fierce mind—a super-naturalist of sorts. His most famous text has a title that is the exact opposite of where Franklin is going. The title is *Sinners in the Hands of an Angry God*, the whole Puritan theology, with its sense of human weakness, human guilt, the severity of the moral world, the severity of the divine world, essentially a very sort of repressive theology. We're going to run into it in a big way when we look at *The Scarlet Letter* of Hawthorne.

All of this is a kind of dominant theme in American thinking at exactly the time that Franklin comes around. Now, Franklin is Edwards' opposite on every front. Franklin is the Yankee, journalist, scientist, naturalist, and businessman. I'd like to say, "Rotarian and diplomat." He's a man who is absolutely a secular figure—if we want to think of Edwards as a figure interested in the divine. People have often seen these two as a very striking and emblematic pair. The traditional view is that Edwards points back to the Puritan past, whereas Franklin points forward to the future. That's a traditional view, but that view has been under fire at different points.

After World War II in particular, there was a lot of interest in the Puritans. There was a revaluation of the contribution that they made to American intellectual life—Jonathan Edwards, but other great Puritan writers and leaders as well. I say after World War II because that was a time, given the kind of slaughter and carnage that took place in that war, where people took a harsh look at Franklin's form of progressivism—his optimism—and it looked a little thin, looked a little flat. His faith and reason didn't really seem to bear up very well in the light of contemporary events. He had his critics even before that. The French novelist, Balzac, once said, "Franklin, inventor of the lightning rod, the republic, and the hoax." William Carlos Williams, who really disliked him, said, "Our wise prophet of chicanery, a perfect pattern book for would be Yankees and cute businessmen." When I was at graduate school at Harvard that was when Perry Miller, who was the very great author on the Puritan tradition, was still alive and still teaching. Miller, I think, sort of led, not the fight against Franklin, but the fight for Puritans and for Edwards, and the critique of Franklin's optimism. It was thought to be a facile kind of optimism.

The reason that I'm alluding to all of that is that Franklin is a serious figure. He really requires that we rethink him. This sort of Edwards/Franklin contrast is useful, but it only goes so far. The list of achievements that I promised is a way of spelling out the career and what this man did. If we're going to say he's a self-made man, let's listen to what he made. He was born in Boston in 1706. We're calling him an American writer and, of course, there was no America in 1706. He didn't think of himself as an American. He was an English colonial. His stock was from England—his family—and so that's what he thought. He was a loyal subject of the King. He was born in 1706 and he was apprenticed to his brother James, a much older brother. There were many children in the family, in Boston, in the printing business, which was the business that he stayed with for most of his life. At 12, he was apprenticed. He's remarkably precocious. He starts writing ballads very early. He reads widely. In 1721—that's at the ripe old age of 15—he starts his own newspaper, *The New England Courant*, and he starts writing essays. He knows he's so young that no one is going to take these essays seriously, so he writes them under pseudonyms—which is something he's going to do a lot during his life—and gets them published. People think that distinguished adults sent them in, and so these things start getting published, and they are very elegant essays. You can't believe that a 15-year-old is writing these things.

In 1723, he bolts from Boston. He's tired of working for his brother. His brother apparently has been very harsh to him, according to what he says. He resents that. He sort of runs away from home—more or less. He sails to New York, which is an incredible thing to do at that time because that's a big voyage, from Boston to New York in 1723. Then he goes on to Philadelphia, which is where he's going to make his career. Even at the age of 18 in Philadelphia, he impresses the people that he meets. He meets the governor of Philadelphia, Governor Keith, who was much taken with him and makes great promises—which Keith is not going to keep—about the connections that he is going to make possible for Franklin. Franklin goes to London on the strength of those promises in 1724—again an 18-year-old crossing the ocean, going to London, with nothing but promises from Keith that "These are the people in London that you will meet." There's a wonderful description that Franklin gives of waiting at the boat to get all this information from Keith, these letters to introduce him to people—letters of introduction. He realizes on the boat, of course, that that mail is kept elsewhere. Then he begins to realize this isn't going to happen. But, he's young and the world is open. It's in front of him. He's heading to London. It's no problem.

He finds employment in London—in printing—very quickly. Again, at this tender age, he begins to meet the leading British intellectuals. He starts to publish articles in Britain. In 1726, he returns to Philadelphia, and that's when he begins to establish himself even further in printing. He is named, in 1730, "The Official Printer of Pennsylvania." Here come some of the things. He creates the first subscription in the United States, in 1731. He starts publishing *Poor Richard's Almanac*, under another pseudonym—he calls himself Richard Saunders and publishes this almanac. He starts that in 1732. He's 26 years old. This he continues to write and publish until 1757, for 25 years. This is the first American bestseller. It's read all over the United States.

He organizes the Union Fire Company in 1736. He becomes the postmaster for Philadelphia in 1737. He's the official printer for New Jersey in 1740. He designs the Franklin fireplace, the Franklin stove, in 1741. He proposes the idea for the American Philosophical Society in 1743. He starts his experiments with electricity in 1745. He organizes the Pennsylvania Militia in 1747. He publishes a document that founds the Philadelphia Academy in 1749—which two years later becomes the University of Pennsylvania. He creates the bill to found the Philadelphia Hospital in 1751. He performs his famous kite experiments, proving that lightning is electrical, in 1752. He designs a flexible catheter for his brother John in 1752, because John has bladder stones.

Hear that list of things? This man is like a prodigy. He's working in three or four different areas at once and simply making things that have never existed before, socially, politically, and scientifically. He starts getting recognition. He gets an honorary MA degree—Masters degree—from both Harvard and Yale in 1753. He's appointed the Postmaster General of North America. He's elected to the Royal Society of London in 1756. He's then elected the agent, the representative, of Philadelphia, or Pennsylvania, to England, and represents the colony there in 1757. Then he moves to London where he spends most of his remaining years, with a significant return later in the 1780s. In England again, he's kept his friends from the early days, and he makes new ones. He becomes acquainted with major intellectuals, scientists, and politicians. He gets the honorary doctorate from the University of St. Andrews in Scotland in 1759 and from Oxford University in 1762.

Now, we're at the time, of course, where the hostilities start to break out between England and the colonies. That happens for the next decade. Franklin works incessantly in the area of political negotiations. He tries to represent the colony, particularly vis-à-vis issues of taxation. He continues, at the same time, to make scientific discoveries. He publishes further. He starts his *Autobiography* in 1771. He's in his mid-60s when he starts writing his autobiography. It's for his son to see what his life was like because, at this point, he's an extremely well known figure. He starts to critique slavery and starts to become an abolitionist in 1772. He has a very active and volatile set of experiences being the agent for the colonies in the English Parliament. There are some tempestuous moments where he's publicly humiliated by the Parliament because he's been involved in leaking information back in Pennsylvania—or Massachusetts, as well.

In 1776, after working ceaselessly to prevent the war, Franklin thinks of himself, as I said, as a colonial. He wants to prevent this war. He's writing, right up to the moment of the war, documents about the possibility of this not happening, of maintaining the peace. Nonetheless, when he sees that it's inevitable, that it won't happen—that there just can't be reconciliation—he, of course, is one of the signers of the Declaration of Independence. People laughed and said that, the only reason that Jefferson was elected to write the Declaration instead of Franklin was that Franklin would've put jokes in it. He's one of the chief negotiators of the war effort. He then is sent to Paris, where he lives, in order to borrow huge sums of money from the French in order to support the American war effort and then to pay bills after the war. He is one of the chief negotiators for creating the peace after the Revolutionary War. He's one of the signatories of that. He witnesses two of the first manned balloon flights in 1783. Someone asked him, "What use is that?" His answer is wonderful, "What use is a newborn baby?" he said.

He returns in 1785 to Philadelphia. He has been called, and it makes sense—it's not an exaggeration—the most famous private citizen in the world at that point. This man comes from nothing. He works then to abolish slavery. He is a Pennsylvania delegate to the Constitutional Convention. He argues for extending the vote. He is one of the chief architects of the notion that the House and the Senate would have different forms of representation, by some only two and then others by population. He continues to write his autobiography. He dies in 1790. Now, that's quite a career. He really is one of the great heroes of the Enlightenment. He's a colossus.

Of course, our concern is predominantly with literature. What sort of an intellectual figure is he? What sort of a portrait does he offer of himself? Well, there's a lot of wit in Franklin. *Poor Richard's Almanac,* I think, warrants that we at least consider a few of its notations, partly because we've all grown up with them. Franklin is in our bloodstream, whether we know it or not. We just don't know that it comes from Franklin. Have you ever heard this, "Early to bed and early to rise makes a man healthy, wealthy, and wise?" You know who said it? Poor Richard did. There are other ones as well, "God helps them that help themselves." Right on! "Don't throw stones at your neighbors if your own windows are glass." Well, he rephrased that one a little bit. "Creditors have better memories than debtors," classic Franklin. Here's one you don't know, "He that lives upon hope, dies farting." That's not bad either. I'd never heard of that one before.

So Franklin is both in and out of our system. That is, a lot of his stuff we have heard. We've grown up with it. We were taught it. Some of his Poor Richard's sayings are really quite provocative. "A plowman on his legs is higher than a gentleman on his knees." That's an interesting comment given the kind of political events that are going to come and about the creation of America. There's also a certain amount of wit in the autobiography itself that I think is worth signaling in a few passages, because I think that they have a certain humor to them. This is about Franklin, who started out young as a committed vegetarian—or a person who wasn't going to eat fish in any event—and talks about being becalmed off of Block Island on a boat:

> Our people set about catching cod, and hauled up a great many. Hitherto I had stuck to my resolution of not eating animal food, and on this occasion consider'd, with my master Tryon, taking every fish as a kind of unprovoked murder, since none of them had, or ever could do us any injury that might justify the slaughter. All this seemed very reasonable. But I had formerly been a great lover of fish, and when this came hot out of the frying-pan, it smelt admirably well. I balanc'd some time between principle and inclination, till I recollected that, when the fish were opened, I saw smaller fish taken out of their stomachs; then thought I, 'if you eat one another, I don't see why we mayn't eat you.' So I din'd upon cod very heartily, and continued to eat with other people, returning only now and then occasionally to a vegetable diet.

Then his conclusion,

> So convenient a thing it is to be a *reasonable creature*, since it enables one to find or make a reason for everything one has a mind to do.

So it's important to know that Franklin has a certain amount of wit, a certain amount of irony, and a certain amount of self-sarcasm as well. This wit stood him in good stead. This wit strikes me as a central ingredient of his career. He was a fabulous success every place he went. As I've told you, as a young man, intellectuals were drawn to him; scientists were drawn to him. There are wonderful stories about his exploits in Paris. He's a man in his 60s and 70s speaking gallant French, wooing these women. The French are enamored of him. There's Benjamin Franklin, the representative from the United States in Paris, and he absolutely creates a storm of attention. There're all kinds of rumors about love affairs and this, that, and the other. He was a terrible husband, by the way. He more or less abandoned his wife Deborah, and they hardly saw each other over the years. That's a kind of sad story. In terms of his public persona, in terms of his achievements at being a social lion, it's really quite astounding.

Autobiography is really the great American story. It's the story that he wrote about his achievements, about his life. One thing that it demands contrast with is one of the several great autobiographies in the 18th century. One of the greatest and most well known ones is *The Confessions of Rousseau*. We read *The Confessions of Rousseau* as a text that tells us about the underside of the Enlightenment, not that Rousseau was a criminal. But it is a very powerful pre-Romantic document about the private life, the intimate life, of Rousseau, the kinds of things that are not in the public record. That's why Rousseau wrote it. You don't find that in Franklin. One critic once said Franklin appears, and I quote, "To be the only person in American history without an unconscious." He's only the record—he is the public record.

I think it's important to understand that this is very 18th century-like itself. It's Rousseau who's exceptional, Franklin is demonstrating over and over in 18th century thinking. Rousseau is our modern figure. We have trouble understanding Franklin here. That public and private go together. That there is no private sanctuary where real life is—which is what Rousseau thought and which many of us think—and that the public is something else. Franklin believed in the public story. He believed in participation. He saw no conflict whatsoever between individual freedom and belonging to groups, membership, participation—being part of a collective effort. That again is an 18th century virtue. Self-determination does not lead to opposition in Franklin's view.

He also felt that this story—which we know about his life because of what he wrote—deserved people's reading it, and he tells his son, but he knows that others will read it too, about his humble origins, about running around Boston and running around Philadelphia as a young man trying to establish himself as a printer, in light of the subsequent achievements that he has made. He feels that this is going to be a useful story. This is the American story. This is *Horatio Alger*. This is *The Great Gatsby*. This is a self-made man. This is the myth that brings people from all over the world to the United States. Here is a place of freedom where you could, in fact, become everything you're capable of. It has nothing to do with class, origin, or who your family was. It has to do with your own pluck, your own brilliance.

Franklin writes as well, in *Autobiography*, about the need to be indirect, the need not to always put yourself forward when you have projects that you want to get done. He's very smart about that. He said every idea that was crucial for him to get approved, he made look like it belonged to other people as well. He learned to temper all of his remarks. He learned not to say "I believe," but rather "It's possible to see it this way." He always agreed with people first, even when he thought they were fools, in order later to get his ideas across. The man is a consummate politico in this sense. He knows how to make things happen. He's wise about vanity.

He's most famous to us as an 18th century moralist of the Enlightenment stamp. He believed in moral behavior. I contrasted him with Jonathan Edwards. He doesn't believe in fire and brimstone, but he believes in moral behavior. He believes that we can control it. He sets forth the principles for doing just that. Those are the features of his work that I think are some of the most remarkable things. "It's about this time," he writes in *Autobiography*, "that I conceived the bold and arduous project of arriving at moral perfection." You could only write this in the 18th century, "moral perfection." "I wish to live without committing any fault any time." Okay, how are you going to do that? Well, "Let me create a list of 13 virtues, the key virtues, and I will live by them." I want to read them to you.

> Temperance: Eat not to dullness; drink not to elevation.

> Silence: Speak not but what may benefit others or yourself; avoid trifling conversation.

> Order: Let all your things have their places; let each part of your business have its time.

Resolution: Resolve to perform what you ought; perform without fail, which you resolved.

Frugality: Make no expense but to do good to others or yourself; that is, waste nothing.

That, of course, he's become famous for.

Industry: (equally famous) Lose no time; be always employed in something useful—cut off all unnecessary actions.

Sincerity: Use no hurtful deceit; think innocently and justly, and, if you speak, speak accordingly.

Justice: Wrong none by doing injuries or omitting the benefits that are your duty.

He goes on to others.

Moderation.

Cleanliness: Tolerate no uncleanness in body, clothes, or habitation.

Tranquility.

Chastity (major one here): Rarely use venery—that's his word for fornication, procreation—venery but for health or offspring, never to dullness, weakness, or the injury of your own or another's peace or reputation.

Humility: Imitate Jesus and Socrates.

These are his virtues. He also designs a weekly scorecard. It's a real scorecard. Each week, he's going to consecrate to one of these virtues. He puts down the amount of time—or rather the offenses for that week—every time he offends against the virtue that he's promulgating that week. He figures that, in 13 weeks through the 13 virtues, he can fundamentally clean his act up. He can make it work. He can get moral perfection. He also writes out a wonderful sort of scheme of employment, that is to say, "How you're going to spend every day?" It's a chart or a graph. It gives the hours from 5:00 in the morning until 4:00 at night, about what you're supposed to be doing. It starts with the morning question, "What good shall I do this day? "The Evening question is, "What good have I done today?" This is not surprising; it's logical. Then, of course, there is the list of all the things he's supposed to do.

It's easy not to like this. One of the most famous dislikers of this was D.H. Lawrence. I'd like to read you just a little bit of that, to get a sense of what the kind of posturing might look like in Franklin. Franklin also devises the essentials of the every known religion, the great universal religious creed. That is that there's one God, who made all things, that he governs the world by his providence, that he ought to be worshipped by adoration, prayer, and thanksgiving, but that the most acceptable service of God is doing good to man, the soul is immortal, and God will certainly reward virtue and punish vice either here or hereafter. That seems to make sense. That's a very 18th century view of things. That's not really a raving enthusiastic view.

That's the kind of thing that Lawrence couldn't bear. "At the beginning of his career, this cunning little Benjamin drew up for himself a creed that should satisfy the professors of every religion but should shock none. Now wasn't that an American thing to do?" Lawrence says.

'There's one God who made all things.'

(But Benjamin made Him.)

'That He governs the world by His Providence.'

(Benjamin knowing all about Providence.)

'That He ought to be worshipped with adoration, prayer, and thanks-giving.'

(Which cost nothing.)

'But-' But me no buts, Benjamin, saith the Lord.

'But that the most acceptable service of God is doing good to men.'

(God having no choice in the matter.)

'That the soul is immortal.'

(You'll see why, in the next clause.)

'And that God will certainly reward virtue and punish vice, [either] here or hereafter.'

Lawrence:

> Now, if Mr. Andrew Carnegie, or any other millionaire, had wished to invent a God to suit his ends, he could not have done better. Benjamin did it for him in the eighteenth century. God is the supreme servant of men who want to get on, to produce. Providence. The provider. The heavenly storekeeper.

Lawrence also rewrites, I think hysterically, the 13 virtues. He takes each one of them: temperance, silence, and order.

> Temperance (Lawrence): Eat and carouse with Bacchus, or munch dry bread with Jesus, but don't sit down without one of your gods."

> Silence: Be still when you have nothing to say; when genuine passion moves you, say what you've got to say, and say it hot.

What do you think Lawrence is going to say about Chastity?

> Never 'use' venery at all. Follow your passional impulse, if it be answered in the other being; but never have any motive in mind, neither offspring nor health nor even pleasure, nor even service. Only know that 'venery' is of the great gods. An offering-up of yourself to the very great gods, the dark ones, and nothing else.

See, Lawrence is the perfect opposite, the dark Romantic mythic opposite to Franklin, the secular thinker, the man with the rules of moral conduct. That's why I think Lawrence is a kind of useful figure to bear in mind. Now, despite the kind of send off that Lawrence offers us—and that other people have offered us—Franklin remains a remarkably potent and important figure. He really is the giant of the 18th century, perhaps only rivaled by George Washington. He's one of our great American icons, literally. You see him—there is the Franklin Fund—you see his picture. He stands for prudent investment everywhere in the United States. He's on the one hundred dollar bill. He really has "made it" in that sense. We can't forget him. He's there. We see him. We're reminded of him constantly. It is also the case that it's appropriate to see him. He loved to be seen. He sat probably for more portraits than anybody in the 18th century.

He's wonderfully perspectival, it seems to me as well, in his writing. He understands something about different points of view. That's why I said that he learns to submerge his own ego when he wants to get something across or he wants to have a particular point made into law or made into a doctrine. He knows not to say "I." He understands, in a kind of intuitive way, that everybody is ruled by their own visions, their own sense of things. He knows how to go with that. That, to me, connotes a kind of elasticity that is quite remarkable. It's easy to think of him as sort of pompous and inflated, the kind of thing that I think Lawrence has in mind. Yet, I think he's supple. I think that he knows and understands points of view. It's not an accident that he writes under pseudonyms. That comes naturally to him. Why not be Poor Richard or write under other names? That is because he can think under other names. He can see the world from other angles. I think that's part and parcel of his work in abolitionism. He wants to overthrow slavery, partly because he is able to see his way around that to see that slaves are also humans, and that this is not in keeping with a democratic culture. This, of course, is happening almost a century before the Civil War.

He is a brilliant organizer and negotiator. As I have said, he bequeaths us with the greatest myth story that we have in this country, which is the success story. People didn't talk about success stories before the late 18th century. That just wasn't a concept, that the individual could make it big in society, independent of origins or background or class or wealth. This is a modern notion and it is an absolutely central ingredient of American thinking. Franklin not only writes about it, but also "is" it. He is our first great example of it. This is "The American Way" then, the dream of success and everything that goes with it, that the material life can be just fine. It doesn't mean because you are successful in your secular life that you're somehow cheating on God or robbing the afterlife. For Franklin, there is something splendidly harmonious in his view of things, and that these things fit together. You serve God best by exploiting and developing and contributing your talents to the world, so that the material life is okay. Success is okay. Happiness is real in Franklin. I don't think Jonathan Edwards could've understood that happiness is real and is a serious virtue.

Some writers cast a shadow over all that follows. Franklin, I'd like to say, and others have said this too, "Casts a light." He casts a light. If you think of the wonderful experiments with lightning, that he snatches light from the heavens. He snatches lightning from the heavens and he gives it back to us in electricity. That is a form of Prometheus, who stole fire from the gods and gave it to men. Franklin is our Prometheus.

Lecture Three
Washington Irving—The First American Storyteller

Scope:

Although Washington Irving is no longer fashionable in American Studies circles, and although his work remains known largely because of two short stories, those stories, "The Legend of Sleepy Hollow" and "Rip Van Winkle," are American classics. Many of us have grown up with them. They were part of the folklore for children's movies of yesteryear, and they are with us still. But the significance of Irving's work goes beyond nostalgia. These two tales speak to us of the early Republic, of the growing pains and anxiety that must have accompanied the momentous shift from English colony to independent nation. "The Legend of Sleepy Hollow" reveals something of the *malaise* the author felt about the bustling, industrious society that America was becoming. In the classic showdown between Ichabod Crane and Brom Bones, Irving sketched an American crossroads, a choice between the goblin-haunted, past-driven schoolteacher and the brash, up-and-coming, muscular realist—which one will win the girl? But "Rip Van Winkle" is assuredly Irving's true claim to immortality, and this story of a man who falls asleep for 20 years seems indeed to escape the law of time, for it haunts us still with its mystery. Once we realize that Rip sleeps precisely through the American Revolution, the story begins to bristle with cultural overtones. Yet its deepest riddle has to do with the strange vision and potion that caused Rip to sleep in the first place, and this question is inseparable from Rip's own odd temperament, his refusal to grow up. It is a prophetic American hang-up.

Objectives: Upon completion of this lecture, you should be able to:

1. Explain how "The Legend of Sleepy Hollow" partakes of America's "Wild West" tradition.

2. Summarize the religious and cultural sources Irving drew on to describe Rip Van Winkle's trip to the mountaintop.

3. Explain how Rip Van Winkle's dilemma is particularly American.

Outline

I. Irving is something of an eclipsed figure in American Studies today: his writing and his education are profoundly Anglophile in character because he spent much of his life in England, courting the famous writers and noblemen of his day. Thus, he hardly seems to be an "indigenous" figure. Yet, because he is writing in the early years of the 19th century, at the beginning of the American experiment, his work sheds an interesting light on the cultural anxieties of the young nation.

II. "The Legend of Sleepy Hollow" (1819) is one of Irving's enduring stories, familiar to many of us in both illustrated book and film forms. This charming story has much to teach us about the new America.

    A. Sleepy Hollow itself is presented as a sort of refuge from the bustling America, a haven where "romance" is still possible.

    B. Ichabod Crane, the famous schoolteacher, functions as artist in Irving's scheme.

        1. Crane is shown in unflattering colors—as a grotesque figure, ravenous in his hunger for material success.

        2. Yet he is also characterized as "our man of letters," as "traveling gazette" for Sleepy Hollow, which unmistakably casts him as a writer, even as an intellectual.

        3. Ichabod is also a storyteller, but of the Cotton Mather school; i.e., of the past stories of witches and demons. This marks him as backwards looking.

    C. Ichabod's challenge, as Irving articulates it in "Wild West" fashion, is: Can he establish himself? Marry Katrina? Defeat his rival?

    D. Brom Bones, Ichabod's rival, has a cultural interest of his own, given the dynamics of early American culture.

        1. Rowdy, strong, brash, and fearless, Brom Bones personifies a figure that will be known as the "b'hoy," an American original of sorts, who challenges all niceties and pieties. Bones is actually referred to in terms that forecast Teddy Roosevelt: a "rough rider."

2. Bones is also the man who fights phantoms and boasts of encountering the infamous, legendary Headless Horseman.

E. In Irving's showdown, the two males "duke it out" by replaying a scene of legend. But Bones is able to best Ichabod by taking charge of the event, by scripting it so perfectly that he becomes the artist, impersonates the Horseman, substitutes a pumpkin for a head, and routs his rival. A new era is at hand, and we see the classic exchange: Ichabod Crane disappears from the scene, but the legend of his encounter with the "ghost" is born.

III. "Rip Van Winkle" (1819) is unquestionably Irving's greatest claim to fame. Although this is a story that most Americans are familiar with, it is doubtful that we have thought through its odd particulars.

A. We all know that the hero has fallen asleep for 20 years, but under what circumstances?

1. The event that Rip has slept through is, of course, the American Revolution. Irving is again telling us something about this new America, a country now liberated from England and embarking on its own path. We may wonder how appetizing this new country is for the author.

2. What changed in the 20 years during which Rip slept? Irving sketches for us a new realm of politics, a new landscape.

B. We recognize, in Rip's visionary experience on the mountaintop, a classic variant of religious epiphany, or illumination.

1. Rip, summoned by the strange figures he sees bowling and drinking, experiences a classic initiation: serving the gods, entering their world.

2. Watching the figures bowl and drink is tantamount to watching the gods at play, and Irving has included references to Barbarossa, Charlemagne, Odin, and Thor. Moreover, the specific "play" itself, Bowling and Thunder, can also be seen as a form of erotic sport.

3. The unanswered question in Rip's encounter with the gods is: Why are they so "grave"? Is this a Christian punishment? Are they harbingers of death? Irving furnishes a number of explanations later, in the story and in the notes.

C. Why is Rip singled out for this strange initiation and experience? How does Irving characterize this odd protagonist?

    1. We see that Rip is no less than the eternal child: he frequents children, and he shuns responsibilities of all sorts.

    2. It is also no accident that Rip is no soldier; we may indeed wonder what kind of gun he is carrying.

    3. Rip does not do "family duty," we are told, and with that notation we may unpack still further the sexual dimensions of this fable. It is no surprise that Rip is ultimately happiest at the "male club," separated from women altogether.

D. We would expect the protagonist of such an "initiation" story to be altered by his experiences. How is Rip changed by the vision?

    1. America is altered in powerful political ways; even nature is altered, as Irving's language suggests. But Rip remains unchanged.

    2. The rusty fowling piece that he carries with him down the mountain fits in perfectly with his new life, a life without wife or "family duty" of any sort.

    3. Irving's story can be read as a leap into male menopause, whereby all the earlier indices of sexual threat are finally removed.

E. Rip's momentous return to the village is arguably Irving's most fascinating touch. The setting is entirely changed, the family Rip earlier sired has grown up, and Rip undergoes what can be seen as a crisis of identity.

    1. Being confronted with his grown-up son, also named Rip, with a grandson as well, Rip "unravels" and experiences an existential collapse; can we not speak of the fissured self?

2. The mobile setting that Rip encounters upon his return, especially the inn that seems to come and go, appears virtually surrealist in its implications, looking forward all the way to Hitchcock's "Psycho."

F. The legacy of "Rip Van Winkle" is rich and various, and we are still working our way through it.

   1. Hart Crane invokes, in "The Bridge," Rip as "the muse of memory."

   2. James Joyce's hero, Leopold Bloom, is memorably figured as Rip Van Winkle: the work of time is seen as the corrosion that besets married life.

   3. Rip Van Winkle is particularly present and accounted for in our upcoming literary performances among the American classics.

      a. Thoreau's performance in moving to Walden Pond can be seen as ambivalent: Face reality or flee reality?

      b. Melville's Captain Delano, "Benito Cereno," will display the frightening dimensions of the childlike vision.

      c. Tom Sawyer and Huckleberry Finn, our most famous literary children, make us wonder if avoiding adulthood is an American vocation.

      d. Hemingway's Jake Barnes, of *The Sun Also Rises*: emasculated male, is a bitter version of Rip's fate— that is, fit only for men.

      e. Faulkner's Quentin Compson, in *The Sound and the Fury*, expresses Irving's chief theme, albeit in a tragic key: you cannot grow up.

   4. The universal warning of Irving's story goes beyond literature altogether: Where has life been? How did we lose it?

Readings:

Essential: Irving, "The Legend of Sleepy Hollow" and "Rip Van Winkle" in *History, Tales and Sketches* (Library of America, 1983)

Recommended: Young, "Fallen From Time" in *Visions and Revisions in Modern American Literary Criticism* (Dutton, 1962)

Topics for Further Consideration:

1. Summarize how "The Legend of Sleepy Hollow" is a parable about the "new" and the "old" America.

2. Explain why Rip Van Winkle sleeps for 20 years.

Lecture Three—Transcript
Washington Irving—The First American Storyteller

This is Lecture Three, which is going to be devoted to Washington Irving. Irving, I would like to suggest, is our first important storyteller. There are people who wrote before Irving. He wrote a great deal. He published a lot. He lived a long life. We don't read most of his work, but there are a couple of things that he wrote that are quite important, and I think are in everybody's minds as part of the American canon. Two short stories: one, "The Legend of Sleepy Hollow" and the other, "Rip Van Winkle." I'd like in this lecture to sketch a little bit—not really much—but to say a little bit about his career and particularly his status today, which is, I think, really dubious. Then, I would like to suggest why I feel he's important, what his work tells us about young America. He is writing, after all, around 1819, 1820—an interesting time.

He really does precede the great Transcendentalists'—Emerson, Thoreau, and Hawthorne—earlier work. All of that's coming in the 1930s, 10 to 15 years after Irving. He's unfashionable today. People don't pay much attention to him in American studies, particularly in an atmosphere in which people are very interested in reclaiming a number of texts—slave narratives—texts that come from other groups. After all, America was a diverse place at this point, and there were lots of different kinds of writing.

Irving is, for many people, impossibly Anglophile. His prose looks British. It doesn't really look American; certainly, doesn't have the kind of twang and the pungency that you find in Emerson and Thoreau, and that comes to culmination in Whitman. Moreover, Irving's own career is really very international and cosmopolitan. He learned lots of languages; he knew German, he knew French, and he knew Spanish. He translated materials from these languages. He lived a great deal of his life in Europe, in exalted places. He had important diplomatic positions. He was a friend of the high and mighty. He met major writers. At the age of 20, he goes to Europe and he meets Madame Distále and Baron von Humboldt. He has important friends in Washington, like Dolly Madison. He meets Walter Scott, who was the great figure at the time. He immerses himself in Spanish history. I said he's the friend of the powerful, as well. He's a friend of Martin van Buren. He becomes a very good friend of John Jacob Aster, one of the first very powerful rich Americans.

It's a career that seems to take place in foreign courts, in elegant places. This is about as far as you could get from writing the story of slave narratives or writing a kind of indigenous American tale. Rather, it seems to be a career that has a kind of international flavor to it. Yet, for all these reasons probably, the two stories that I'm interested in, "Rip Van Winkle" and "The Legend of Sleepy Hollow," —and that I think all of us are interested in—have a very interesting perspective about America, about new America, about America as it was changing in front of Irving's eyes—as it had changed already.

I'd like to start with "The Legend of Sleepy Hollow," the story of Ichabod Crane and the Headless Horseman, the story that was published in 1819 and that we all know. We knew it as children, or at least when I was a child. We saw cartoon versions of it—it's one of the earliest memories I've got. We were scared of that; but it was before we got today's kinds of monsters. I mean, the Headless Horseman really did the job in those days. But, we certainly weren't encouraged to think about what kind of place Sleepy Hollow was. Irving has thought about it. Sleepy Hollow is just what the name says, it's a sleepy hollow. It's out of the way. It's not part of the bustling American mainstream, which is what he says,

> I mention this peaceful spot with all possible laud for it is in such little retired Dutch valleys, found here and there…that population, manners, and customs remain fixed, while the great torrent of migration and improvement, (and I want you to hear it, the bustling new America that's happening) which is making such incessant changes in other parts of this restless country, sweeps by them unobserved.

It's a kind of place that's secluded. It's a place that's a byway. It hasn't been touched by what is then the noisy—and I think for Irving unpleasant—disturbing progress of America. This is also an opportune place for romance. This is the place he talks about, "A drowsy, dreamy influence that hangs over the land." And he talks about the "witching power" that exists there. He talks about the aberration of a figure on horseback without a head, the story of the "Hessian trooper whose head had been carried away by a cannonball" and who continues to haunt the place. You get the feeling this is the only kind of place where that could happen; this legend could still be kept alive.

Well, our protagonist is Ichabod Crane. I want to suggest that Ichabod Crane—something I never thought when I was young and first knew this story—is really outfitted. He's a grotesque character. He's described as a "huge feeder." He has the "dilating powers of an anaconda,"—doesn't really sound very attractive. Nonetheless, he is your representative intellectual. He's the schoolmaster. Irving calls him "Our man of letters," I'm quoting. Irving calls him "a kind of traveling gazette" as he goes from place to place telling stories. These are the features of the artist. These are the features of the writer. These are the features of the intellectual—grotesque, caricatural. Comical though he is, he seems to also have a kind of symbolic status in this story. He, himself, is a lettered person. He particularly tells stories that go back to Cotton Mathers' history of New England witchcraft. He's a creature of the past, is what I want to say. He's a creature who represents an America prior to this bustling, businesslike world that's coming into reality in front of him. This is a man who is an intellectual, who goes back to Cotton Mathers, to witchcraft, who seems to be therefore to kind of have a kinship with legend, with romance, with fancy as well.

The story, in some sense, is about his fortunes. Whether he can succeed in implanting himself. He wants to marry Katrina, who is the daughter of this wealthy Dutch farmer, and this is the kind of classic, comical project. Is this man going to be able to marry this women, et cetera, and then establish himself? Again, in equally classic fashion, he has a rival. His rival, you may remember, his name is Brom Bones. Actually, his real name is not Brom Bones, that's a short, it's Brom Van Brunt—Dutch name—but they call him Brom Bones. I want you to hear how he's described, because he's the polar opposite of Ichabod.

> He was famed for great knowledge and skill in horsemanship, being as dexterous on horseback as a Tartar. He was foremost at all races and cock fights; and, with the ascendancy which bodily strength [always] acquires in rustic life, was the umpire in all disputes, setting his hat on one side, and giving his decisions with an air and tone that admitted of no gainsay or appeal. He was always ready for either a fight or a frolic; but had more mischief than ill-will

in his composition; and with all his overbearing roughness, there was a strong dash of waggish good humor at bottom.

So Brom Bones is a new kind of type, unlike Ichabod Crane who represents the old Cotton Mathers, the learned figure. Brom Bones is the new roughneck kind of figure. They have a name for this in early 19th century literature; he's called the b'hoy—like boy—but, b'hoy. The b'hoy has a counterpart who was the g'hal, the gal. You see text with these kinds of figures. This is not just esoteric, because I think that Brom Bones is, in a sense, the forbearer of people like Melville's Ishmael in a book that says, "Call me Ishmael," as the very first line of it, and with the kind of brashness and the kind of sauntering nature of Ishmael, or Walt Whitman, who was a "rough"—is what he calls himself—a cosmos. All of that, I think, is part of this same type, the same figure that Brom Bones is. That's that kind of "shootout" story we've got here. This is the rivalry, the contest, between these two people, Ichabod Crane and Brom Bones. Which one is going to carry the day?

Brom Bones looks, as I said, towards Whitman; he looks towards Melville. You have a phrase "Brom Bones and his gang of rough riders." He looks towards Teddy Roosevelt; he looks towards a whole American ideal of tough guy, macho, of ready to fight it out, of quickness of wit and quickness of strength. That's what Ichabod has to fight, and he's going to lose that battle. In that showdown, through the use of the Hessian Headless Horseman, we're going to see Ichabod Crane bested, and in interesting ways. Brom Bones, as you may remember, already brags about the fact that he's encountered this Headless Horseman and already beaten him a couple of times. Then he will set off another encounter for Ichabod. And, it's after they're leaving the big party from Katrina's father that he is followed by this man—or he sees this huge figure on horseback.

It's interesting the way Irving writes this because, as Ichabod tries to get out of there on Gunpowder, his horse, the other horse and rider stick with him; it's like a dark double in certain ways. Which of these two is going to carry it? And, there's only room for one of them. That's the old line, "there's only room for one of us in this town." I think that's what this story is about. You may remember that what happens is, that the Headless Horseman throws his head at Ichabod, and that's when Ichabod is routed. It hits him in the head, one head hitting another—it's really a head game of sorts, this story—and he falls off his horse and they all go whizzing by. All they found the next day is a pumpkin, of which was the head. This is reality over romance, in some sense. It is a reality using romance. Brom Bones using a pumpkin and touting it as the head of the horseman, throwing it at Ichabod, and Ichabod disappears.

The story ends where we're told that Brom Bones marries Katrina. That is the comic result. That's the rhythm of comedy. All comedies end in marriage. That's the continuation of the community. Ichabod is gone. Of course, he's not gone. His legend is born. You really get a kind of classic duality there. Yes, Brom Bones carries the day, wins the battle, but Ichabod wins the war, in some sense. The legend, itself, stays. So, it's a nice story. I think it already suggests—in the defeat of this person, Ichabod, in the victory of a man like Brom Bones—a kind of hesitancy, a kind of malaise on the part of Irving about what this new country is becoming. It's a little bit uncouth. It's a little bit rough. He's not sure how much he likes it.

I say that partly as a lead-in to "Rip Van Winkle," which is his most celebrated story and which is a story that really is lodged, I think, in all of our minds. We've all heard it. We can't forget it. For the most part, we think of it as a story about a man who simply slept for 20 years, which is true. I mean, obviously that is the fundamental event in the story. It's shocking when you go back and read it, or think about it, as to what he slept through. He slept through the American Revolution. He slept through the single founding event in the history of this country. Now, that cannot be an accident. Something symbolic is happening here that this man sleeps through this particular event. When he wakes up, the country ain't the same; he doesn't know what's happened to him, what's happened to the place. "The village was altered; it was larger and more populous. There were rows of houses he'd never seen before. Those, which had been his familiar haunts, had disappeared. Strange names were over the doors; strange faces at the windows; everything was strange."

And it's not just strange, he's not so sure that he really likes it. "There was, as usual, a crowd of folk about the door, but none that Rip recollected. The very character of the people seemed changed. There was a busy,"—and now you remember that language about Sleepy Hollow—"there was a busy, bustling, disputatious town about it,"—that's what Irving doesn't like—"instead of the accustomed phlegm and drowsy tranquility." "In a place of these, he said,"—the people he was looking for that he remembered 20 years earlier—"a lean, bilious-looking fellow, with his pockets full of handbills, was haranguing vehemently about rights of citizens," Now this doesn't make sense to Rip Van Winkle, what are they talking about rights of citizens? "Elections." What's an election? Why are you having an election? He doesn't know what this means. After all, he fell asleep when this belonged to good old King George! "Members of Congress, liberty, Bunker Hill, heroes of '76," and other words, which were a perfect Babylonish jargon to the bewildered Van Winkle.

All of our great mythic events in the founding of this country are Babylonish jargon to him. It doesn't make sense to him. It's not clear what Irving thinks of this great myth either, of these great legendary events. Rip has missed all of that. That's what he slept through. King George, whose emblem he's looking for when he goes to the inn that he used to hang out at, he thinks he sees it.

> He recognized on the sign the ruby face of King George, under which he had smoked so many a peaceful pipe; but even this was singularly metamorphosed. The red coat was changed for one of blue and buff, a sword was held in the hand instead of a sceptre, the head was decorated with a cocked hat, and underneath was printed in large characters, GENERAL WASHINGTON.

Who was this? What's going on? What happened to Rip? To use the language of the Bible—or the language of Martin Luther King—he went to the mountaintop and he had a vision. He had a vision, and what did he see? Well, it's a vision really that is close to an initiation. He goes into the mountains one day, and he hears voices calling him, "Rip Van Winkle, Rip Van Winkle," and they want him to come. He doesn't understand what it is. He sees these strange figures. He sees first, a strange man who makes signs for him to approach, and there's no real language, just signs here. Then he hears strange things like "rolling peals, like distant thunder, that seemed to issue from a deep ravine, or cleft." And then we later learn that these rolling peals are, in fact, these strange people playing at nine-pins, bowling. Strange mythic figures that he sees—they are described as mythic—one of them had a face that consisted entirely of a nose, another looked like a "Commander." They had beards of various shapes and colors. All we see are these people playing this strange game.

"Nothing interrupted the stillness of the scene, but the noise of the balls which, whenever they were rolled, echoed along the mountains like the rumbling peals of thunder." He looks at them, and they make signs for him to come and to "wait upon the company." He does, and then he has to help carry these kegs and pour liquid into these flagons, then he is going then to drink of the liquid, and that's what's going to put him to sleep. But what has he seen? What is this strange vision?

If you've read any Joseph Campbell, or anything like that, this is a clear myth of initiation. He's been initiated into some strange thing. People have argued, in very interesting terms, that this is a description of the gods. That he has seen these weird figures who have come back, and he's watching the gods at play, at sport. They are rolling the nine-pins and creating the thunder. These are the nature gods. We know that, at the end of the story, Irving, himself, is going to suggest that this was the ghost or the return of Hendrick Hudson, who has come back. That's what they're going to tell him in the story, itself. Even that, is not the only explanation. One person says, "his father had once seen them in their old Dutch dresses playing at nine-pins in a hollow of the mountain, the founder of the river and country, Hendrick Hudson."

Then, in the note that is written afterwards, Irving talks about the myths that have grown up in the Catskills. It's been a region, he said, "always full of fable. The Indians considered them the abode of spirits, who influenced the weather." He adds as well, "They were ruled by an old squaw spirit, said to be their mother." So you've got Hendrick Hudson, squaws, Indian gods and goddesses. All of this seems to be brought into play. People have done myth studies of this short little text and they have found references to Barbarossa. They have found references to Charlemagne. They've also found references with the thundering to the Nordic gods, to Odin, and Thor in particular—the god of thunder.

It may not seem perfectly obvious to you, that they said that this is not just the play of the gods, but this is the erotic sport of the gods—that these balls and ninepins, that these gods at play—that he has somehow witnessed some erotic power, some erotic game. The gods are doing their exploits. I'm going to tell you why that is an interesting reading. Why was Rip Van Winkle selected for this particular initiation? What is it that Irving has told us about Rip Van Winkle? Well, listen to some of this description of Rip:

> The children of the village, too, would shout with joy whenever he approached. He assisted at their sports, made their playthings, taught them to fly kites and shoot marbles, and told them long stories of ghosts, witches, and Indians.

Or we learn about Rip: "He was a kind neighbor, and an obedient henpecked husband." That talked about his meekness of spirit.

Rip Van Winkle is described as not only henpecked and playing with children, but he is very childlike, himself. He would do odd jobs for other people, we're told. "Do such little odd jobs as their less obliging husbands,"—for the women in the village—"would not do for them." In a word, "Rip was ready to attend to anybody's business but his own; but as to doing family duty, and keeping his farm in order, he found it impossible." Now, I don't want to sound too Freudian to you, but as to doing "family duty," there is an implication of conjugal duty, and he's not up for that, as it were. He doesn't do things like that. He "carries a fowling-piece on his shoulder," but one begins to wonder about this fowling-piece that Rip has. "His children were as ragged and wild as if they belonged to nobody." So what Rip is not, is much of a father or a husband. That's the way he's characterized as a kind of childlike figure.

He's not a soldier. He doesn't have much of a gun. I think that his greatest desire is to really hang out with other men, not to be much involved with women, not to be much involved with those kinds of responsibilities. Listen to some of the imagry of this story: "Times grew worse and worse with Rip Van Winkle as years of matrimony rolled on. A tart temper never mellows with age, and a sharp tongue, (that's his wife's tongue) is the only edged tool that grows keener with constant use."

I want you to hear something threatening in that. This tongue, which is a tool that grows sharper and sharper. He hangs out with other guys "frequenting a perpetual club of the sages, philosophers, and other idle personages of the village." So there's something childlike about him, and that really makes sense if you think of this as an initiation story. He's going to come of age in a big way—go 20 years.

Well, when he wakes up everything has changed. I've already read to you how the government had changed, how the affairs of the country had changed. I want you to see as well that the landscape has changed. He wakes up and it's "a bright sunny morning." It's like "Morning in America," as they would say. It really is. The new country has established itself. "The birds were hopping and twittering among the bushes, and the eagle was wheeling aloft, and breasting the pure mountain breeze." There had only been a gully when he made his way up to this place, but now he finds "a mountain stream foaming, leaping from rock to rock, filling the glen with babbling murmurs as if nature, itself, has been rejuvenated." Rip has grown old. Nature and the country have grown young. There's something interesting that's going on here.

He is old and he finds that his things are old. "He looked round for his gun, but in place of the clean well-oiled fowling-piece, he found an old firelock lying by him, the barrel encrusted with rust, the lock falling off, and the stock worm-eaten." A rusty fowling-piece. What I want to say is that he leaps into male menopause at the end of this story. He goes back home. His wife is mercifully dead, so he's not going to have to deal with her anymore. "Having nothing to do at home, and being arrived at that happy age when a man can be idle with impunity, he took his place once more on the bench at the inn, and was reverenced as one of the patriarchs of the village." He's out of business as a kind of functional male in any other sense. He used to say, "there was one species of despotism under which he had long groaned,"—and he's now talking about George III—"and that was petticoat government. Happily that was at an end; he had got his neck out of the yoke of matrimony."

Well, he is free at last. This has worked well for him, and yet the return to this village has also been traumatic. The most interesting lines in this story have to do with Rip's return. You recall he doesn't know that he slept for 20 years. He doesn't recognize any of the people. He doesn't recognize the place. He cries out in despair, "Does nobody here know Rip Van Winkle?" And here's how Irving writes it,

> 'Oh, Rip Van Winkle,' exclaimed two or three, 'To be sure! that's Rip Van Winkle yonder, leaning against the tree.' Rip looked, and saw a precise counterpart of himself, as he went

up to the mountain: apparently as lazy, and certainly as ragged. The poor fellow was completely confounded.

It's like he's been replicated. It's his double. "He doubted his own identity, and whether he was himself or another man." Now, this is a bit existential for a text from the early 1800s.

> In the midst of his bewilderment, the man in the cocked hat demanded who he was, what was his name? 'God knows,' exclaimed he, at his wit's end; 'I'm not myself—I'm somebody else—that's me yonder—no—that's somebody else got into my shoes—I was myself last night, but I fell asleep on the mountain, and they've changed my gun, every thing's changed, and I'm changed, and I can't tell what's my name, or who I am!'

This is pretty strong stuff. This is about a complete fissuring of identity, a kind of implosion that all of the contours collapse here. He doesn't know who he is. The setting in the story really bears that out; that the inn is no longer an inn, it's now called a hotel. It's described in a very intersting kind of way. It's Doolittle Hotel, it's the kind of place that you'd be happy at. But nonetheless, it's described as "A large rickety wooden building with great gaping windows, some of them broken and mended with old hats and petticoats. Instead of a tree that used to be there, there's a tall naked pole,"—and there, too, I hear something insistent—"a tall naked pole with something on the top that looked like a red nightcap, and from it was fluttering a flag." And we realize it's the stars and stripes, and that he doesn't know what that is.

Well, what I've given you is a kind of Freudian reading of this story, as well as a kind of mythic reading. That he watches the play of the gods because that's the play that's been alien to his life forever. He starts as a child. He ends as a child—as an old child. He has totally circumvented his adult sexuality. He circumvented marital responsibility. He has never been, in any conscience sense, a father—a responsible person. He ends up being the storyteller of his own past, as he sits there as a so-called patriarch at the end of the story. What does all this mean?

We just finished hearing about Benjamin Franklin. Benjamin Franklin is the great American story of the self-made man. He is the great American story of "Anyone can be president." He is the great

American story of tireless achievement, of assertion, adult responsibility in the difficult arenas of business, government, and politics. Here's the other American story. It's the story of escape. It's the story of opting out. It's a story of maturing by remaining a child. It's Peter Pan, Peter Pan who slept 20 years.

This is the other story that is going to be, I think, an American classic. It's also about memory. Hart Crane, the poet, referred to "Rip Van Winkle" as the muse of memory. James Joyce in *Ulysses* cites "Rip Van Winkle" when he's talking about Leopold Bloom. Leopold Bloom's story in *Ulysses* is a story of a man who has discontinued sexual relations with his wife, and who can only remember a time when they were vital. So Joyce, I think, rightly makes use of this story. It's in Bloom's memory, or in his stream of consciousness, as a game when they were children. "Rip van Winkle we played. Rip: tear in Henny Doyle's overcoat." This is Joyce. Rip means to rip somebody's clothes, so he's going to do it that way. "Van: breadvan delivering. Winkle: cockles and periwinkles. Then I did Rip Van Winkle coming back. She leaned on the sideboard watching. Moorish eyes." He's remembering Molly when she was young. "Twenty years asleep in Sleepy Hollow. All changed. Forgotten. The young are old. His gun rusty from the dew."

That's a story of impotence. It's a story of the death of love, the failure of love. It's a story of vitality and passion only existing in the past. It's a perfect reference back to Rip Van Winkle. So this has been, as it were, a potent story in the history of this country and the history of literature, not just American literature. But, it's particularly in American literature that the dream is of escape, the dream is of getting clear from social responsibility, sexual responsibility. It's a male dream. It's a dream that absolutely punctuates American literature as much as Thoreau's *Walden* is a heroic text. It also can be read as an escapist text. Man goes to woods, hangs out.

We will talk about Melville's fabulous story "Benito Cereno," about a childlike captain, Captain Delano, and what it means to remain a child—how you could get things wrong if you never grow up. It's about two boys' adventures, Tom Sawyer and Huckleberry Finn—particularly Tom Sawyer—Americans who never grow up and were forever children. The dream is about looking for the territory where you might be able to remain a child. That's how *Huckleberry Finn* closes. In its darker permutations, it's Jake Barns in *The Sun Also Rises*, who is emasculated and hence cannot be active sexually. It's Quentin Compson in *The Sound and the Fury,* who will go into the Charles River as a student in college, killing himself, because he cannot grow up. This is a story about failure to grow up. "Rip Van Winkle" is about sleeping through your life. It's about losing your life. Where is your past, as well as, where is your future?

Lecture Four
Ralph Waldo Emerson Yesterday—
America's Coming of Age

Scope:

Emerson, the guiding spirit of American Romanticism, lays the groundwork for a key tradition in American thinking and writing in his *Essays,* written from the 1830s through the middle of the century. His status as essayist and philosopher in mid-19th-century American culture is unmatched by any other figure. Even though his "rank" in the pantheon has had its ups and downs, his influence is still with us, not only in our literature, but also in our lives and values. Chief architect for the American belief in the empowered self, Emerson has a range and reach that are not easily mapped or subject to simple definition. We will begin with his early wake-up calls, claiming the need for a new and original American literature, liberated from the influences of Europe and the past. Then we will focus on Emerson's single most influential essay, "Self-Reliance," to see how complex and destabilizing these ideas really are. Finally, we will consider Emerson's richest and most challenging essay, "Experience," in which he sketches a view of ideology and perception that is shockingly close to contemporary thinking about knowledge, truth, and even self as both mediated and constructed.

This examination of the beginning of Emerson's career will focus on a few central early texts—including "Nature" (1836), and "The American Scholar" (1837)—as well as on the seminal ideas about American literature found in "The Poet" and "History." The predominant thesis that emerges here is no less than an American "declaration of independence" in all arenas—culture, literature, and ethics.

Objectives: Upon completion of this lecture, you should be able to:

1. Describe the cultural liberation advocated by Emerson in essays such as "Nature

2. Summarize Emerson's notion of the universal man.

3. Explain Emerson's opinion of scholarship.

Outline

I. There are many problems with the term "transcendentalism," but Emerson and Thoreau, our transcendental "Romantic" poets, are crucial to grasping what American literature becomes by the time of Whitman. Emerson's beginnings are not earth shaking, and few could have predicted the work that he would produce.

A. Emerson was only a middling student at Harvard College (1817–1821), graduating at the middle of his class.

B. In chronic poor health, Emerson nonetheless attended Harvard Divinity School.

C. In 1829, Emerson married Ellen Tucker, herself ill with tuberculosis, and this crisis continues until her death in 1831.

D. Unable to believe in or preside over the sacraments, Emerson resigns ministry in 1832; at this point, his true "education" begins.

E. Emerson traveled to Europe and met the great writers Coleridge, Wordsworth, and Carlyle, whose rousing work particularly moved him.

F. Emerson moved to Concord, began to lecture in Boston, and was quickly recognized as the guiding light among the new group called Transcendentalists

II. "Nature" (1836) was Emerson's great breakthrough text, and with it he immediately acquired an audience of the best and the brightest.

A. Emerson announced essentially a new beginning for America; the political liberation was established, but the cultural one was yet to come.

1. The first order of business Emerson prescribed was a radical break from the past, an imperious need to create an indigenous American cultural agenda and manner.

2. Emerson, doubtless influenced by the great Romantic poets such as Wordsworth, envisioned a new relationship between man and nature. His most famous image of himself experiencing the wonder of nature is the "transparent eyeball," characterized by a complete erasure of the lines separating self and environment.

3. Emerson especially articulated the need for a new language, an idiom that would be commensurate with the revolutionary tidings he had in mind. In this regard, Emerson's theories proved quite influential for subsequent writers.

B. Emerson's concept of language is a mix of cultural and linguistic notions.

    1. Nature itself is seen in semiotic terms, in that all things are understood as *signs* for other things; hence, "words are signs of natural facts" and "nature is the symbol of spirit."

    2. Emerson's material linguistics, have real implications for the writer because they mandate a search for "original language," for the word that most closely describes the thing.

    3. The project is strategic: the "right" writing allows you to tap into power, to recover the indwelling force that is linked to words.

    4. This noble view of utterance issues a challenge of the writer: to describe reality by "opening it up," to "speak" the riddle of the sphinx.

    5. Emerson's view of writing is expressed as a challenge for America: to open up "facts" of our indigenous new landscape and way of life and to liberate the magic and promise of America by capturing its essence and strength in the right language.

III. Emerson's famous speech at Harvard, "The American Scholar" (1837), is seen as a wake-up call to the country's young intellectuals.

    A. American achievements in the political arena have not been matched intellectually or culturally, Emerson contended. It's time for America to measure up.

    B. We must apprehend "Universal Man," Emerson argues, by which he means that divisions of labor and specialization blind us. In this sense, he offers a preview of Karl Marx.

    C. We must go beyond scholarship as well, because the university's slavish and passive attitude can never produce a creative energy of its own.

    D. We must fashion an indigenous American language, to be found in our countryside and among our simple people, close to the earth and nature.

E. In a remarkable passage, Emerson takes on the "subjectivism" of his time and claims that we must go beyond introspection, beyond self-searching, and enter the world of facts and deeds.

IV. Emerson is the prophet of American cultural independence.

    A. "The Poet" (1846) is Emerson's chief statement about the literary agenda of the future.

        1. Poetry is our commonwealth, Emerson claims, by which he means literally that it enriches all of us and makes us wealthy as a nation.

        2. America is the great new poetic subject. The writer is to make us see what is timeless and enduring in our moment, just as Homer and Shakespeare did in their moments.

        3. We need a vehicular language, Emerson said, so that the poet may move his audience, and bring them into his vision of America. For this purpose, the old locutions of the past would not do.

        4. In a famous paragraph, Emerson called for the poet of the future, outlined the poet's duties, and virtually predefined what happened in 1855 when Whitman published *Leaves of Grass*.

    B. In "History" (1841), Emerson articulated still further the revolutionary work in culture that had not yet been accomplished.

        1. Emerson is our poet of the New World. He claimed that America must move into its estate, must carry out its great mission of freedom and democracy.

        2. Emerson argued that our contemporary "actual knowledge is cheap," that we needlessly settle for routine notions and second-hand knowledge.

        3. Setting the new American agenda is the ultimate goal of Emerson's essays: he is the great encourager, the visionary who claims that we have not begun to take or to give our measure as a nation.

        4. Both Twain and Faulkner developed a language that was inspired by Emerson.

Lecture Four—Transcript
Ralph Waldo Emerson Yesterday—
America's Coming of Age

This is Lecture Four, and it's the first of three lectures on Emerson. It's going to be followed by three lectures on Thoreau. Now we usually think of Emerson and Thoreau as the great duo for what is called American Transcendentalism. In my opinion, that term is an unfortunate term—even though it has its truth—because it connotes a kind of arid, boring, pontificating body of tenets that belongs as much to the church as it really does to literature.

There's a lot of truth in that: Emerson does pontificate and Emerson was in the church. What that terms misses, and what I think needs to be restored to our understanding of transcendentalism and to Emerson and to Thoreau, is the extraordinary beauty and quickness of their language. That these are "our" Romantic poets—Emerson and Thoreau are Yankee versions of what England has in Wordsworth and Keats and Shelly. That is a claim that I'd like to try to substantiate by looking carefully at the language of Emerson's *Essays*. I'll quote a lot because Emerson is a spellbinding writer. His words and images, his metaphors, grab us, and they make us think differently about the issues that he's talking about, which is really what he has in mind.

When we think of these figures, Ralph Waldo Emerson, and the whole slew of mid and late 19th century American writers—Henry Wadsworth Longfellow—there is something mellifluous here. They're all three names. They all roll off the tongue: James Russell Lowell, Oliver Wendell Holmes, and William Jennings Brian. There's something, it seems to me, a bit pompous, inflated—indicating museum pieces. What vitality or excitement could they have for us? That too is a reason for taking a good look at Emerson, settling in, chewing a bit on his language, on his ideas.

He's the great guiding light, it seems to me, of American literature. He's not the first figure in our course. Certainly, there were American writers or writers producing literature in this country before it's called America, such as Franklin and Washington Irving. Emerson is the moment where I think American literature becomes American.

In our sequence of lectures on Emerson we're going to try to pay attention to several facets of his work. We'll pay attention to the particular *Essays* that he wrote in the third and fourth decades of the 19th century. The first lecture is going to be devoted predominantly to Emerson's views on language, which will lead us to an understanding of Emerson's seminal role in American poetry.

Emerson is really the entry to Walt Whitman. He articulates the ideas about poetry that Whitman is later going to actualize. Emerson is most known for his great essay called "Self Reliance." If he's not known for it, we certainly know that the idea is a central tenant in American values. It was important too when Emerson stated these beliefs; new then, and every bit as much with us today. It's synonymous with what's America. It's an essay, however, that is much more complex, provocative, and destabilizing than we ordinarily think. I'll close with a lecture on Emerson's later essays, not really the end of his career, but more mature essays. In particular, I will discuss an essay called "Experience," where Emerson appears to have gone full circle and begins to raise the series of questions about notions of self, of reliance, and of identity, that will be puzzling to us; that are very much in keeping with some of the most modern contemporary ideas about identity as something that is constructed—not something that is innate—or about consciousness, subjectivity itself being made up of things that are outside in the culture and not simply in hearing within us.

There's a range in Emerson's work, and it's a range that is rewarding when one looks at it. It doesn't cancel out the earlier positions, but it adds a certain amount of depth to them. In a sense, it problematizes them. No one looking at Emerson's beginnings would have thought that this would be the great visionary writer in the American tradition, or that he would lay down the key notions about self, about our relation to nature, about the need for creating a new kind of language in literature. You wouldn't have thought that. He was a middling student. He went to Harvard, but it wasn't quite as difficult to get into then as it is today. His health was not great. He, nonetheless, went to Harvard divinity school after he graduated from the college in 1821. He marries early. He marries a woman, Ellen Tucker, who is ill with tuberculosis; as I said, his own health was poor. She dies in 1831, and there is a feeling that this is his first encounter with tragedy, with death, and with loss.

It happens at a time when he is beginning to rethink a number of key ideas in his own formation. In particular, he resigns the ministry in 1832, predominantly because he has grave questions about the sacraments—about conducting communion—and feels that he is no longer able to fully believe in this or to do this. At that point, Emerson goes to Europe, and he meets—in England—a host of terribly important writers. He meets John Stuart Mill. He meets Coleridge. He meets Wordsworth, and he meets Thomas Carlyle, whose brand of fiery enthusiasm and iconoclasm much appeals to him. He then moves back to the United States, and he moves to Concord, and he begins to give his famous lectures—famous then, famous now. People have written about what it was like to hear this man talk. He was spellbinding and hypnotic. They didn't always understand—they often didn't understand. People of serious intellect said afterwards, "I was absolutely mesmerized listening to him, but I don't really think I understood a word he said." They didn't mean that as a criticism. They felt like there was a kind of higher logic being expressed here, something that grabbed them that was not easy to spell out in the kind of discursive terms people were used to.

He published, in 1836, his breakthrough first text, which is *Nature*. It's an appropriate term for it. This is the text where Emerson fully breaks with the past and announces a new regime. I'll read you the first lines of *Nature*.

> Our age is retrospective. It builds the sepulchres of the fathers. It writes biographies, histories, and criticism. The foregoing generations beheld God and nature face to face; we, through their eyes. Why should not we also enjoy an original relation to the universe? Why should not we have a poetry and philosophy of insight and not of tradition, and a religion by revelation to us, and not the history of theirs? Embosomed (listen to the language here) for a season in nature, whose floods of life stream around and through us, and invite us by the powers they supply, to action proportioned to nature, why should we grope among the dry bones of the past, or put the living generation into masquerade out of its faded wardrobe? The sun shines to-day also. There's more wool and flax in the fields. There are new lands, new men, and new thoughts. Let us demand our own works and laws and worship.

So this is a kind of clarion call. It's a trumpet blast that says, "We need to create our own culture." Emerson proclaims a kind of remarkable fusion with the natural world in one of his most famous—or infamous really—references. He describes himself as a "transparent eyeball." There's actually a cartoon at the time, which lampoons him and shows him as a huge eyeball,

> Standing on the bare ground—my head bathed by the blithe air, and uplifted into infinite space,—all mean egotism vanishes. I become a transparent eyeball. I am nothing. I see all. The currents of the Universal Being circulate through me; I am part or particle of God.

Now this vision, this experience, requires a particular kind of language to make it happen. In this first publication, *Nature*, Emerson lays down some remarkable principles about language. In particular, he sounds like a theorist—sounds like a modern linguist. He numbers them one, two, three; here are his three principles. "Words are signs of natural facts." This is beginning of American semiotics. "Words are signs of natural facts. Particular natural facts are symbols of particular spiritual facts. Nature is the symbol of spirit." Can you see the dance that's involved there, the traffic that's involved in these notions? Everything signals to, is a conduit for, something else. Words are not just linguistic codes or notations. They are the signs of natural facts; they send us back to the world of nature. "But that the world of nature is not simply phenomenal material, it is also spiritual, because natural facts are symbols of spiritual facts, and nature is the symbol of spirit." Emerson illustrates this model by doing a certain amount of etymology.

He explains that the words that we have all derive back from physical properties. He says "right" means "straight;" "wrong" means "twisted;" "spirit" primarily means "wind;" "transgression" is "the crossing of a line;" "supercilious," is "the raising of the eyebrow." He talks about our consistent use of metaphor here. We say the "heart" to express emotion; the "head" to denote thought. We are always on the move in Emerson's words. He wants us to understand the fluidity here. Sometimes, he moves towards what looks like a search for original language, and this has its own politics. For example, he writes that, if we want to find really vivid language, we go back to people who are not cultured or cultivated. It's this I quote, "Which gives that piquancy to the conversation of the strong-natured farmer or backwoodsman, which all men relish." And he adds, "These facts may suggest the advantage which the country life possesses for a powerful mind over the artificial and curtailed life of cities." This is an article of Romantic thinking. As you go into nature you find the people who live in nature and, lo and behold, their very language is going to be closer to these material and spiritual origins that are so important to him—that he wants to make more visible.

There's also a view of power, and that's one of the most exciting features in Emerson's work. If we use the right language, if we learn how to speak right, and learn how to see right, and learn how to think right, we find ourselves initiated into an extraordinary power system. It's the power that flows through nature. It's in a sense, a way of accessing the enormity of forces that otherwise we seem to have lost sight of. I quote again:

> We are thus assisted by natural objects in the expression of particular meanings. But how great a language to convey such pepper-corn informations! Did it need such noble races of creatures, this perfusion of forms, this host of orbs in heaven, to furnish man with the dictionary and grammar of his municipal speech? Whilst we use this grand cipher to expedite the affairs of our pot and kettle, we feel that we have not yet put it to its use, neither are able. (And here comes this really brilliant, beautiful phrase) We are like travelers using the cinders of a volcano to roast their eggs.

That here is this remarkable machinery, this great powerful engine, is nature, which is the physical world, and we're using it for the most reductive purposes. We haven't yet seen its power and its majesty. Tapping into power is going to be a kind of lifelong concern of Emerson. He regards writers as people who have always been interested in doing that, and he actually says that the writer—not just the literary writer but the philosopher, the oracle—is someone who has always, in Emerson's words, "sat at the feet of the sphinx."

He says, "There sits the Sphinx at the road-side, and from age to age, as each prophet goes by, he tries his fortune at reading her riddle." The sphinx is there. The great mystery is there. The conduit of power is there. The challenge is for us to be able to read it, to decode it, to make it somehow accessible to our own people, to our own peers. In keeping with the same linguistics, he ends up by saying, "A Fact is the end or last issue of spirit." A fact is the end or last issue of spirit. Things are not just things, they're the culmination of an entire spiritual process. Opening up facts then is the great requirement here. Open up facts. Open up this material world and see the spiritual wonders that are in it.

> All that Adam had, all that Caesar could, you have and can do. Adam called his house, heaven and earth; Caesar called his house, Rome; you perhaps call yours, the cobbler's trade; a hundred acres of plowed land; or scholar's garret. Yet line for line and point for point, your dominion is as great as theirs, though without fine names.

There's a kind of emancipating goal here, a liberating goal here: come into your estate, recognize that what you're doing is your estate, that it has grandeur and it has scope beyond anything that you have dreamed of. So, as I said, this was a clarion call, this essay "Nature." Young people read this and said, "This is magnificent. This is a kind of stupendous opening." Older people read this and were not happy that this was a very subversive kind of talk. The real subversive talk was the one that Emerson gave the next year at Harvard. He gave the Phi Beta Kappa oration in 1837, and this talk has now come down to us as the "American Scholar." Emerson was not invited back to Harvard for 29 years after giving this talk. But imagine how young people in 1837 heard this.

Emerson really tells it straight about what's wrong with the United States in terms of culture. He's talking about the literary achievements of a country that's very enterprising and bustling on the material front. He says, "Thus far, our holiday has been simply a friendly sign of the survival of the love of letters amongst the people too busy to give to letters anymore." Like, literature's not dead. It's survived; but I mean, nothing's happening.

> Perhaps the time has already come when it ought to be, and will be, something else; when the sluggard intellect of this continent will look from under its iron lids, and fill the postponed expectation of the world with something better than the exertions of mechanical skill. Our day of dependence, our long apprenticeship to the learning of other lands, draws to a close. The millions that are around us rushing into life cannot always be fed on the sere remains of

foreign harvests. Events, actions arise, that must be sung, that will sing themselves.

And so, in this speech, Emerson begins to spell out the need for there to be an indigenous American idiom, an indigenous American message. This speech is rich in other implications as well. It's also a speech that strangely has implications that are almost Marxist in terms of his critique of the division of labor, of the smallest of the lives that Americans lead. "Man is not a farmer or professor or an engineer but he is all. Man is priest and scholar and statesman and producer and soldier." He goes on to say that, in our current scheme, we have somehow been reduced to the particular role that we play, rather than realizing that this is just a part of our large repertory. Man is thus metamorphosed into a thing—into many things. "The planter, who is man sent out into the field to gather food, is seldom cheered by any idea of the true dignity of his ministry." He goes through other professions that people have and it's the same kind of critique that Marx is doing just a little bit later, that labor has become mechanical, that people have lost the sense of the worth or dignity or scope or ultimate meaning of their own work. Emerson is making a comparable argument here.

Emerson also—here I think the people at Harvard were uncomfortable—puts down scholarship. He says, "Meek young men grow up in libraries,"—this is given at Harvard— "believing it their duty to accept the views which Cicero, which Locke, which Bacon, have given, forgetful that Cicero, Locke, and Bacon were only young men in libraries when they wrote these books." Get out of the libraries. Use the writers but get out of the libraries and do your work. Embrace the present. In a remarkable sequence, Emerson acknowledges that his is an age of introversion, introspection, and he asked, "Should that be evil, should that be a restraint?" He cites Hamlet's "sickly aura with the pale cast of thought," that we seem to be locked into subjectivity. Is this so bad then?

The response he gives is, "Let us move into our own land, our own culture; let us get beyond this introspective cast. The literature of the poor, the feelings of the child, the philosophy of the street, the meaning of household life are the topics of the time. It is a great stride." He says: Why do we spend our time copying the models of the past?

> I ask not for the great, the remote, the romantic; what is doing in Italy or Arabia; what is Greek art, or Provencal minstrelsy; I embrace the common, I explore and sit at the feet of the familiar, the low. Give me insight into to-day, and you may have the antique and future worlds. What would we really know the meaning of? The meal in the firkin; the milk in the pan; the ballad in the street; the news of the boat; the glance of the eye; the form and the gait of the body.

Emerson then lays down the laws for a new kind of writing. Writing in America—by and large—prior to that was modeled on European codes, on a class system as well, that fits into the European model, which deals with kings and queens and divinities. All of this is to be rejected for a frank but excited view of our own new democratic society.

Emerson has a very exalted view of poetry itself. That poetry should be not an elitist art form, but a form that brings us into the riches that we ourselves can lay claim to. He says the poet is representative. It's a word that Emerson likes to use—representative. One of his great series is called *Representative Men*. What does he mean by it? "He stands among partial men for the complete man," and listen to this very beautiful phase, "and apprises us not of his wealth but of the commonwealth." All the greatness that you see in Shakespeare and in Dante and in Socrates is your greatness. This isn't their genius only; it allows you to tap into it, and therefore to lay claim to it. This is what expands your estate.

America then becomes a place where this kind of greatness has to be seen, which means we have to rethink what kind of literature we have. Poetry is not just an affair of rhyme verse. "It's not meters, he says, "but a meter making argument that makes a poem." He wants a language, he says, "That is vehicular," that moves people, that promotes this commerce between words and things and things and spirit. He calls for a poet of the future, and these lines read so strangely as we read them a century and a half later because it is an absolute call to Walt Whitman.

> I look in vain for the poet whom I describe. We do not, with sufficient plainness, or sufficient profoundness, address ourselves to life, nor dare we chaunt our own times and social circumstance. ...We have yet had no genius in America, with tyrannous eye, which knew the value of our

incomparable materials, and saw, in the barbarism and materialism of the times, another carnival of the same gods whose picture he so much admires in Homer; then, in the middle age; then in Calvinism.

And here, this next line is perfect Emerson and it's going to be perfect Whitman:

> Banks and tariffs, the newspaper and caucus, Methodism and Unitarianism are flat and dull to dull people, but rest on the same foundations of wonder as the town of Troy, and the temple of Delphi, and are as swiftly passing away. Our logrolling, our stumps (these are the homely particulars of American life in the 1830s) and our politics, our fisheries, our Negroes, and Indians, our boasts, and our repudiations, the wrath of rogues, and the pusillanimity of honest men, the northern trade, the southern planting, (here's Whitman's program) the western clearing, Oregon, and Texas are yet unsung. Yet America is a poem in our eyes; (Whitman would repeat exactly those lines) its ample geography dazzles the imagination, and it will not wait long for metres.

And it didn't have to wait long for meters. This is the poet of the future who's being called here. Whitman actually said, "I was simmering, simmering, simmering, and Emerson brought me to a boil." And, I think that we can understand that when we look at these prophetic lines.

I'd like to begin closing this talk by referring to an essay called "History" where he furthers the view of moving into our estate, of finally taking proper claim, proper ownership of what is ours. "There is one mind common to all individual men," he says.

> Every man is an inlet to the same and to all of the same. He that is once admitted to the right of reason is made a freeman of the whole estate. What Plato has thought, he may think; what a saint has felt, he may feel; what at any time has befallen any man, he can understand.

It's that sense of a grand program, of becoming heir to all of the tradition, but seeing it as it plays in the United States—in America—in this new democratic culture. That's what he calls for, that's what he fails to see around him. He actually uses the term "Our actual knowledge is cheap," by which he says it doesn't have the value that it should have. He claims that we must broaden the horizons.

> Broader and deeper we must write our annals,--from an ethical reformation, from an influx of the ever new, ever sanative conscience,--if we would trulier express our central and wide-related nature, instead of this old chronology of selfishness and pride to which we have too long lent our eyes. Already that day exists for us, shines in on us unawares, but the path of science and of letters is not the way into nature.

Here comes the list of people who are going to bring us to an understanding of nature:

> The idiot, the Indian, the child and the unschooled farmer's boy stand nearer to the light by which nature is to be read, than the dissector or the antiquary.

Move from the libraries, move from the universities, move into the woods, move to the farms, see the young, see the unschooled, understand, hear, grasp the pith of their language, sense the proximity that they have to the vital sources. This is going to be Emerson's legacy, and it is a legacy. This is *Huckleberry Finn*. This is what Twain is going to inherit. This is the idiot in *The Sound and the Fury*, Benjy Compson. Twain and Faulkner are going to find languages—and they will find remarkable languages—that will actualize the promise of Emerson's remarks. This is a proclamation here. This is a "declaration of independence" of a different sort. That's why I've called this, The Birth of American Literature. It says that there "is" an American literature. That's a striking, stunning notion. Most people in the 19th century didn't think that, but it would be an idle claim if we didn't have a whole spate of masterpieces in American literature that actualize—that make good on, fully good on—the promise and excitement of Emerson's theories. So he's the man to contend with, he has had his way.

Lecture Five
Emerson Today—Architect of American Values

Scope:

In Emerson's most famous and seminal essay, "Self-Reliance," we encounter his bold and confident vision of the self. Although our American value scheme is clearly indebted to this vision, we need to grasp the radical implications of Emerson's thinking, especially regarding our role in society, our consistency as selves, and our notions of identity. In particular, Emerson's view of self is immense, almost super-personal, with a kind of reservoir that the individual taps into when he or she is actualized. Likewise, this circuit of power is unsettling in its dictates insofar as we seek to maintain a unified self, since Emerson feels that conformity stifles authenticity.

Objectives: Upon completion of this lecture, you should be able to:

1. Contrast Emerson's and Franklin's notions of self-reliance.

2. Summarize Emerson's attitude toward education.

3. Describe the Emersonian idea of the self and "becoming."

Outline

I. Emerson's most recognized essay, "Self-Reliance," is an audacious program about the risks, strengths, dimensions, and ramifications of selfhood.

    A. The recognizable American religion of self derives in part from Emerson, but there is much that is unfamiliar in this essay. Emerson addresses self predominantly as a kind of energy system that the individual taps into.

        1. He picks up this secular idea, found in Franklin, and converts it into a new type of religion.

    B. All greatness, according to Emerson, is found in self-reliance. The individual never reaches full potential, never gives his or her full measure, unless this final commitment "inward" is made.

        1. Genius, as we see it throughout history, is always the story of self-reliance, of people who religiously followed their own bent.

        2. Genius, as we encounter it, is for us also a form of self-recovery in that it enables us to recover this vital indwelling force and reestablishes our own link in the circuit.

3. Emerson understood genuine self as a new aristocracy, a kind of elitism that all people are heir to, if they have the courage.

C. Tapping into originary power is Emerson's fundamental gambit.

1. Emerson defines this existing source of universal energy as the "aboriginal self," a kind of prior force that we all partake of.

2. Emerson contrasts "tuition" as a clear opposite to "Intuition," and with this preference given to the innate over the learned, Emerson offers a scathing view of the actual results of education.

3. "Perception is not whimsical, but fatal," according to Emerson, because nothing is accidental or external in our modus operandi. The challenge is to take ourselves seriously, to realize that our responses to the world are indices of who we are, and that we must act on this knowledge.

4. Self is bonded to the universe in Emerson's large-framed view so that the predictable solipsism that we might anticipate in a philosophy of self-reliance yields to a large, virtually communal view of self interacting harmoniously with both the outside nature and the inside nature. The "oversoul" is what Emerson names this reservoir of spirit.

D. The most dramatic features of Emerson's essay have to do with the inescapable behavioral consequences of such a philosophy.

1. "Good vs. bad," our traditional Judeo-Christian code, is replaced by the far more intuitive system, "natural vs. unnatural." A new ethics is born.

2. Emerson celebrates nonchalance, spontaneity, and naturalness vs. our cultivated moral code, our learned behavior.

3. Emerson emerges as profoundly, unapologetically antisocial in his tidings because society inevitably entails some form of self-betrayal, or at the very least, self-

neglect. He rejects philanthropy and the "joint-stock company" view of society.

4. Rejecting all foreign models, Emerson issues his famous injunction: Never imitate. Is this model conceivable?

5. Emerson calls into question the utility of any "instruction," particularly as it relates to the imitation of great models. His argument is that these models themselves never studied or imitated anything, but were true to themselves. The educational ramifications of this view are interesting.

6. Emerson's critique of the current American scene is harsh and sweeping: everywhere he looks, he sees slavishness and convention.

7. Although Emerson is thought of as optimistic and "progressive," some of his most scathing comments have to do with our illusion of progress and development.

II. Emerson and the Heroics of Self.

A. Emerson quickly identifies the greatest enemy of self-reliance: our own "fixed" identity. Breaking the prison of fixed identity is the arduous challenge.

1. Emerson's most dazzling pages have to do with the cult of nonconformity, and here he effectively rewrites history as a record of geniuses who have been courageous enough to be true to themselves.

2. Emerson illuminates the conservatism at the core of identity: our need to remain the same. Hence, he attacks the "maintenance" of identity as a key step for liberation. He stresses the importance of being true to one's instincts, as opposed to personal consistency.

B. Emerson posits speech as the most conspicuous index of authenticity—if your language is moldy, your ideas cannot be fresh.

C. In a stunning metaphor, Emerson defines the soul as pure light, and if we are true to it, all is illuminated in a radiance that has no truck with tradition or history.

D. The most arduous task of all, according to Emerson, is learning to live in the present, learning to be faithful to instinct and inner voice at every moment of one's life.

E. Emerson's final doctrine is: The soul *becomes*.

1. This emphasis on "becoming" simply rewrites history, makes all judgments tentative and shifting, makes every life an open-ended adventure. We see here the cubistic Emerson who graphs a new dispensation of knowledge.

2. We should recognize Emerson's arduous, existential view of self for its integrity and difficulty. There is nothing casual or lazy about Emerson's ethics. Being "yourself" is hard.

Lecture Five—Transcript
Emerson Today—Architect of American Values

This is Lecture Five, and in this second lecture on Emerson I want to speak essentially about probably his most famous, most seminal essay, called "Self Reliance." Now self-reliance does not strike us as a particularly revolutionary notion, and that's partially because of Emerson's success, it seems to me. He's helped us to see it as a kind of normal condition of life in this country. Also, I think it's fair to say that Emerson is picking up a kind of confident, secular strain that we already see in the work of Benjamin Franklin. What goes beyond Franklin, and beyond any other writer, is the way in which Emerson is going to convert this view of self-reliance into a religious creed.

That has a particular point to it, because we will see that all other religious authorities, moral authorities, social authorities, are going to be essentially banished. Self-reliance is going to be the great soul-dominating tyrannical creed for understanding how to behave and what life is about. So he's not simply saying, "You should rely also on yourself," he's saying, "You rely only on yourself." Reliance on anything else is misplaced. That's what the thrust of this essay is about, is to show you what it means to rely on yourself, what kind of source that truly is.

One of the remarkable features of this essay is that it simply explodes, I think, our notion of what "self" is that we're relying on. Most of us think of self as essentially located within some core identity of personhood. In Emerson, it weirdly becomes something that is outside us as well as inside us, some large stream or current or force that we tap into when we rely on ourselves. We, in a sense, join the rhythm of the universe, we become most purely, authentically real. There are a lot of politics connected with this. That the notion of the "swollen self," many people regard as one of America's worst gifts to modern culture. We know the statistics about the amount of material goods that Americans consume vis-à-vis the world, et cetera. There's no question that the notion of the "empowered self" takes a beating in a lot of ideological context—and I don't want to minimize that at all. I think that Emerson's essay is not by any means something that we're always going to be comfortable with, but he does go the full route. We will want to think about the charge of the "imperialistic self" as it might relate to Emerson's claims. Emerson, I'm going to be suggesting, expands, challenges, widens our optic on what it means to have a self. He maps it out. He maps out the dimensions. It's like a new continent that comes into view when you read this essay. I want to preface this lecture that way because I feel like "self" seems to us such a familiar concept; it's one that we think we know. In many ways you might say it's the one thing that we think we know, but I don't believe that's the case when you really look at what Emerson has to say about it.

The first thing he claims is that all great people have been self-reliant, that's what they have been.

> Familiar as the voice of the mind is to each, the highest merit we ascribe to Moses, Plato and Milton is that they set at naught books and traditions, and spoke not what men, but what they thought.

That everyone who achieves greatness fundamentally listens to the inner voice, fundamentally rejects, (this is Emerson's view here) the outside voices of other texts, other traditions, other authorities.

Now listen to this phrase here, "In every work of genius, we recognize our own rejected thoughts. They come back to us with a certain alienated majesty." What an extraordinary remark that is, that when we read Shakespeare or Milton or Plato, we recapture something of ourselves. He uses the word "rejected," our own rejected thoughts, and he's thinking that literally—etymologically— they have been thrown from us, but their alienated majesty is now finally brought back home to us. We repossess our own estate through the encounter with great people so that Emerson's view of self is starting to become very capacious and very communal. Lots of folks are in there. They're all helping you to a sense of your own plenitude, a sense of your own reach, a sense of your own resources. It's really a quite remarkable view of things. We ordinarily have too lazy small a notion for it, some inner private core. He's going to blow that sky high. He's saying that it's enormous and that every time something outside comes into us, it helps us to see it, and to expand it. That's how we possess the world. We recover ourselves in attending to genius.

It won't surprise you that Emerson views all of us then as aristocrats. This is an interesting line given the kind of social issues and the very virulent sense of democratic institutions that Emerson subscribed to, and he gives this little fable,

That popular fable of the sot who was picked up dead drunk in the street, carried to the duke's house, washed and dressed and laid in the duke's bed, and, on his waking, treated with all obsequious ceremony like the duke, and assured that he had been insane, owes its popularity to the fact, that it symbolizes so well the state of man, who is in the world a sot, but now and then wakes up, exercises his reason, and finds himself a true prince.

So this is not some exotic fable. This is the kind of aristocracy, majesty, richness, that we are all heir to, and, of course, self-reliance is going to be the strategy. Once again, it's an issue of tapping into power. The power that's there in the world that somehow we have blinded ourselves to. This self then is not in us, as I've said. It's enormous. He coins a beautiful phrase for it. He calls it "the aboriginal self" on which a universal reliance may be grounded. It's there. It's out there. It's in the world. We have to learn to move into it. There are lots of interesting consequences that go here. How do we learn about this aboriginal self? Well, you don't learn about it through books. It's true that the encounter with Shakespeare or Plato may help you, but he makes a very sharp distinction here when talks about spontaneity and instinct.

"We denote this primary wisdom—spontaneity and instinct—as intuition." That's a word we're all familiar with. But listen to the natural opposite of intuition: "Whilst all later teachings are tuitions," intuition versus tuition. Now we think of tuition as a financial term today. That's what you have to pay to send your children to college. He means tuition as everything that you learn versus everything that you—in a sense—tap into, move into, feel in your senses, in your mind, inside of you, not that you locate in libraries or in books. "All later teachings are tuitions." Here again you can imagine that the academy wouldn't be very comfortable with this man because he's constantly saying that the true source of intelligence, wisdom, as well as behavior, is within.

He also adds the line—and this is an astonishing line— "Perception is not whimsical but fatal." Perception is not whimsical but fatal. What we see, what we feel, these are the very attributes of who we are. This is not guesswork. This is not accidental. This is what life has made us, and we better attend to it. We better know what our own machine is, what our own mannerisms are, our own rhythms, our own dance. Perception is fatal. How we look at the world is who we are. Now I stress that because Emerson, in later essays, is going to begin to turn a corner in that sense of the primacy of individual perception.

The self then is bonded to the world. In one famous essay that is called the "Oversoul," the oversoul is like that aboriginal self, it's that large network, that large reservoir that we are part of. He's going to define that reservoir very beautifully in the "Oversoul." He's going to give it a very biological definition. "And this because the heart in thee is the heart of all. Not a valve, not a wall, not an intersection is there anywhere in nature, but one blood rolls uninterruptedly in endless circulation through all men as the water of the globe is all one sea and truly seen its tide is one." Hemingway in *For Whom the Bell Tolls* is going to pick up something of this notion and turn it into a kind of ethos. Here we have an almost biological— the blood flowing—but almost ecological in the sense that we're all connected by some flowing system view.

Again, self would be essentially our connection to it. We think it's our private, single heart that pumps our blood. He's saying there's a larger blood stream that we're all part of. Now, what are the consequences of this? They're amazing consequences. They had to do with how you behave, what rules you observe; and, in a striking formulation, he quite simply inverts the entire Judeo-Christian ethos. "No law can be sacred to me but that of my nature. Good and bad are but names very readily transferable to this or that. The only right is what is after my constitution. The only wrong is what is against it." Good and bad—bye-bye, bible—rejected. They mean nothing. Every culture, every religion, every creed has redefined them. Simply jettison that tired dualism, and say, here's the new one, natural versus unnatural—instinctive versus artificial. What feels right, what is after my nature, as he says, that is the new ethos. That's the new moral code. That's the only code. What is alien to it is evil for me. You can imagine again how any institution of moral or spiritual values—whether it's the church or whether it's the government—is going to have a lot of problems with this kind of ecstatic celebration of instinct, of inner feeling as the only operative code, the only one.

There's something wonderful about the way Emerson just goes the full route. He gives us interesting views about how you achieve this. One of the things that he celebrates, for example, is nonchalance. He suggests that children are, in a sense, the right models for us to follow. They don't worry themselves about dissecting moral issues. They are always—at least he thinks—natural creatures who obey their instinct and move easily through the world and easily within their own circles. He feels that we should perhaps imitate them. We should perhaps try to learn something of the virtues of nonchalance versus cultivation.

It's also, as you can well imagine, the case that this is a deeply anti-social philosophy. The needs of others, the reality of outside codes, outside requirements, the very reality of the world really gets dismissed as irrelevant or perhaps as a nuisance, an annoyance. Emerson can be really quite brutal, and we'll see the same is true for Thoreau. There's something very antisocial in both of these men. Emerson:

> Men descend to meet. In their habitual and mean service to the world, for which they forsake their native nobleness, they resemble those Arabian sheiks who dwell in mean houses and affect an external poverty, to escape the rapacity of the Pacha, and reserve all their display of wealth for their interior and guarded retirements.

It's a kind of interesting extended analogy that the sheiks who dress the outsides of their houses meanly, simply, in homely fashion, and kept all of their splendor and wealth on the inside for themselves— he says this is a figure of life. When we deal with others—when we meet others—we descend, we reduce. Our true riches and glamour and grandeur are inside, that's where it all exists. So he does a lot of "no-no's" in terms of 19th century thinking. He rejects the notion of charity. He rejects the notion of being good to other people.

> Do not tell me, as a good man did to-day, of my obligation to put all poor men in good situations. Are they my poor? I tell thee thou foolish philanthropist that I grudge the dollar, the dime, the cent, I give to such men as do not belong to me and to whom I do not belong.

Don't waste your time giving out your money. It's wasted money, wasted time. It's alien. It's not you. You're not enriching what counts here. He rejects what he calls the "joint stock company" view of society. That's a view that you're going to see again when we come to Melville, because people on board a ship really have reason to think that the world is a joint stock company and that they are intricately related to one another. Not so Emerson. This is all going to be sent away. Now, this model of self-reliance, needless to say, regards all imitation as mistaken. That you don't look at external models.

The very famous line in Emerson is, "Insist on yourself, never imitate." Insist on yourself, never imitate. Now, you may want to ask, is that possible? And in one of the most harrowing stories in the 19th century, Melville's tale of "Bartleby," who was a copyist, Melville is playing with that; about can you, in modern society, avoid imitation? Modern society then being the society of the 1850s. For Emerson, this is not a problem. Likewise, "reject instruction," don't imitate the books that you read either. "Where is the master who could have taught Shakespeare? Where is the master who could have instructed Franklin or Washington or Bacon or Newton? Every great man is unique." He goes on to say, "Shakespeare will never be made by the study of Shakespeare." He has said in one other phrase, "The one thing I have against Hamlet is, that it exists." That is to say, it's out there, which means we're going to try to copy it. Whereas, what we should do is rival it, do something on our own that's of that scale.

Reject foreign models, do not imitate, reject instruction, reject even genius, in so far as it puts a kind of constraint on you and makes you slavish or servile. Emerson is also prepared to reject the frills of his own modern culture. This comes at a time when there's a kind of cheery optimism about American progress. That seems to be an indigenous feature of American society. Emerson can be very caustic about how much we have actually progressed in this day and age.

> The civilized man has built a coach, but has lost the use of his feet. He is supported on crutches, but lacks so much support of muscle. He has a fine Geneva watch, but he fails at the skill to tell the hour by the sun. A Greenwich nautical almanac he has, and so being sure of the information when he wants it, the man in the street does not know a star in the sky. The solstice he does not observe; the equinox he knows as little; and the whole bright calendar of the year is without a dial in his mind.

Now, that's part of the rejections that you have to be in touch with, what's in yourself, and you have to be in tune with that flowing set of forces in the world. I think in that last passage we get a sense that it's the heavens and the stars, as well as the oceans and nature. Self-reliance, as I said, doesn't seem to us to be a revolutionary notion. What I've tried to get at so far is the way in which Emerson expands our view of it, makes us realize the capaciousness of it, that it's outside of us, that it taps in to other forces, that it, in a sense, allows us to reclaim the world.

What I want now to do—after suggesting that this has moral problems, we may offend the operative value systems, the authority systems of any particular culture by being true to this inner instinctual reality—I want now to get at something rather different, which is, I think, one of the most exciting things in this essay, which is how difficult it is to be self-reliant if you're going to go the full route as Emerson does. What are the problems of being self-reliant? And, what Emerson is going to suggest is that we have to rethink our notion of what a self is. Perhaps to give a modern term, of what a personality is, of what an identity is. The most unforgettable lines in this essay have to do with our need for consistency, our need for being more or less the same today that we were yesterday, last week, and last year. This is something that others expect of us. The world expects us to be reasonably the same; but worst still, it's something that we expect of ourselves.

Emerson writes, "The other terror that scares us from self trust is our consistency, our reverence for our past act or word because the eyes of others have no other data for computing our orbit than our past acts." That's all they know of us. They don't know that we are kaleidoscopic on the inside, that we could be anything. They know us by a small number of statements and gestures, our career, our established positions. "They have fixed us," as he says, "They have computed our orbit." It's a remarkable verb, isn't it, written in the 1830s. We are loath to disappoint them. How many times does someone hear, "You're not yourself today?" People tell you that. You want to say to them, "Well, who am I then if I'm not myself?" What they're telling you is, you're doing something that is unlike what you have accustomed us to think you are; but you know that that too, is in you. It's either dormant, you've said no to it up to now—whatever. It's part of your repertory, part of your makeup. What Emerson is going to attack in this essay is the notion of maintaining a self. Maintenance is going to go over the boards here—by the boards.

Instead, he's going to suggest don't give two thoughts to what you were yesterday, five minutes ago even. It'd be hard to give a lecture doing that, but that's what he's going to suggest here. It says about your consistency, "Why should you keep your head over your shoulder? Why drag about this corps of your memory, lest you contradict somewhat you have stated in this or that public place. Suppose you should contradict yourself, what then?" And he then goes on to these famous lines, which are really quite beautiful, "A foolish consistency is the hobgoblin of little minds adored by little statesmen and philosophers and divines." It almost rhymes.

> With consistency a great soul has simply nothing to do. He may as well concern himself with his shadow on the wall. Speak what you think now in hard words, and tomorrow speak what tomorrow thinks in hard words again, though it contradict every thing you said today. 'Ah, so you shall be sure to be misunderstood.' (He says) Is it so bad, then to be misunderstood? Pythagoras was misunderstood, and Socrates, and Jesus, and Luther, and Copernicus, and Galileo, and Newton, and every pure and wise spirit that ever took flesh. To be great is to be misunderstood.

This is something that people were just not used to. I'm not sure we're used to it today. That this notion of being consistent—which is really a way of saying being coherent, having an identity, having a personality—Emerson is quite prepared to rupture that. He's quite prepared to be a merry-go-round, a roller coaster, a kaleidoscope, to be mercurial. He's aware of all of the possibilities that are in him, and they're all real. What he doesn't want to do is to falsify any of them, or to reject them.

So, that sense of maintaining "a self" is one of the worst enemies of self-reliance. To rely on the self is to require a certain amount of courage to be true to your instincts. That's why spontaneity is so important. That's why intuition is valued so much more than tuition. How do you know when people are sincere, authentic, or original? Well, it won't surprise you that one way you figure it out is by their language. "If a man claims to know and speak of God and carries you backward to the phraseology of some old moldered nation, in another country, in another world, believe him not." Okay? If this comes with the old trappings, whether it's biblical or whatever, forget it. That's not in any sense related to the godhead that is in you that you can tap into.

Speech then becomes an index of authenticity. Emerson also speaks of finding the light of the soul. This is an astonishing philosophical line here, "Time and space are but the physiological colors which the eye makes." Melville is going to say something very close to this in *Moby Dick*. "But the soul is light, where it is, is day, where it was, is night. History is an impertinence and in injury if it be anything more than a cheerful epilogue or parable of my being and becoming." What a cavalier remark here. We reject history. We reject the past. The soul is light, and what we want to do is follow soul—follow our soul. It creates reality; it engenders reality; it engenders life; and where it no longer is, is dark. Don't worry about the lessons of the past. Learn to trust the soul to see by its light, to reconceive time and space, which in fact he does. He reconceives time and space. He says that we are trapped. We're trapped particularly in time in this way, that we either postpone or we remember.

We all know it's true. The hardest thing in the world is to live in the present. We're constantly thinking either of what's to come or what has come. "Man postpones or remembers. He does not live in the present, and with reverted eye laments the past or, heedless of the riches that surround him, stands on tiptoe," he says, "to foresee the future." He wants to liberate us from that posture, to learn to live in the present and to see the world around us by the light of the soul. It's not easy to be spontaneous, to be true to one's inner light, one's inner resources. This is all what self-reliance consists of.

I'm going to close this by referring to his really quite, I think, difficult formulation about how this comes back to power and how the soul itself is not a static timeless thing but in fact moves. I said that light moves. What the soul produces is light and where it's not it's dark. This is all mobile.

> Life only avail, not the having lived. Power ceases in the instant of repose; it resides in the moment of transition from a past to a new state, in the shooting of the gulf, in the darting to an aim. (Listen to that wonderful vocabulary: shooting, darting.) This one fact the world hates, that the soul *becomes*.

As I said, this is difficult. What does it mean that the soul "becomes?" Well here's what he says it means. "For that forever degrades the past, turns all riches to poverty, all reputations to a shame, confounds the saint with the rogue, shoves Jesus and Judas equally aside, the soul becomes, God moves." There's a kind of Darwinian evolution here of spirit and of light and of soul, and the past models are past models. They are no longer divine. They're no longer filled with radiance. The soul becomes. I said this is mobile. This is cubistic. This is a way of saying that the world is taking new shape every day. Divinity is moving, metamorphosing, being relocated. We too move with it. That's what it means to live in the now. That's what self-reliance means; to keep attuned, keep in touch with that flow.

Lecture Six
Emerson Tomorrow—
Deconstructing Culture and Self

Scope:

Emerson's philosophy is easily misconstrued as a facile optimism. The Modernists who celebrated figures like Melville and Dickinson, who saw the American artist as a countercultural figure, were not inclined to understand Emerson. Yet his thinking, at its most challenging, looks forward to Nietzsche and Foucault in their view of ideology as social construct, independent of individual choice, even constitutive of individual consciousness. Emerson's supreme accomplishment lies in his essay, "Experience," in which he boldly confronts issues of alienation and mediated consciousness, yet is able to envision at the same time an exciting ethics of freedom.

Objectives: Upon completion of this lecture, you should be able to:

1. Identify some of the modern spiritual descendants of Emerson.

2. Appraise the extent to which Emersonian thought can be considered religious.

3. Explain the Emersonian notion of human freedom and whether it really exists.

Outline

I. Emerson is a neglected, even maligned, figure in American cultural history. His confidence in self-reliance and his revolutionary fervor has led to a view of him as eternal optimist. In the early part of the 20th century, when a number of American authors, such as Melville, Whitman, and Dickinson, were rescued from obscurity, Emerson was disregarded in the literary community.

II. Emerson, when he is seen in his complexity, emerges as spiritual father to Nietzsche and Foucault, as a prophetic figure who had no illusions about the "constructedness" of both consciousness and value systems. Such awareness is all the more remarkable when we consider Emerson's genuine belief in the powers of self.

A. Although Emerson never uses Foucault's term "discourse," he nonetheless articulates a vision of ideology formation that is remarkably modern: the human subject is born into a cultural system that will govern much of what ends up being "thinkable." This is particularly evident in his essay "Circles."

B. Despite his fervent belief in self, Emerson is no less committed to self-cancellation, to a willingness to jettison an "old" self in order to be true to the emerging one.

C. All order, all forms of cogency and definition, can ultimately be seen as the result of circumstances, even as prison-house.

D. There are no "walls" or boundaries in reality; humans construct these "lines" for purposes of definition and demarcation, but they are fictive.

E. Emerson faces directly the necessity of conflict and hate in a world of incessant change because he knows that we cannot tolerate the erosion of our "truths."

F. Emerson's view is astonishingly mobile, and history appears as a kind of dance over time, an evolving play of laws and principles that men persist in thinking immutable.

G. The ultimate Emersonian self, no less than the self's vista, is an ever-shifting kaleidoscope.

H. In answer to the urgent question that emerges in such a vision, the question of "how to behave," or "what to trust," Emerson's reply is stark: abandonment—abandonment to your "nature," with impulses as your only truth.

III. Emerson's future legacy is most richly expressed in his supreme essay, "Experience;" in implicit homage to Montaigne, whose final essay is also "Experience." The American philosopher offers his homely view of our place, both on the planet and within our bodies.

A. Emerson's first law is simple and awful: we are dispossessed, of both self and home. There is no "natural" abode for the self; our somatic and affective lives have a weird independence, an "otherness" beyond our control.

B. The evolutionary rhythm of every life, its changing views and shed skins, suggests the primal law of evanescence and change: there is no originary self.

C. In keeping with the perspectival and subjectivist thinking that starts with Hume and Berkeley, and that undergirds Romanticism, Emerson acknowledges that we see the world through lenses; there is no unmediated vision.

    1. Through these lenses, what we know affects what we see, and events take on meaning and shape for us. It is a carnival, a multicolored world.

    2. One of Emerson's most striking observations is that we "inhabit" a temperament: our affect, our mood, our "humors" (as would have been said at an earlier moment) effectively dictate what we can make of the world.

    3. We are on a treadmill, as well, according to Emerson, because we are doomed to never remain in the same place or to remain the same self, either.

D. Emerson's solution to these matters is tonic; whereas one might expect a kind of blue funk, he is joyous about our freedom.

    1. Rule No. 1 is that life is real, no matter how contingent our categories and concepts are; hence, Emerson urges praxis over theory, especially in matters of education and training the young.

    2. Praxis itself is defined in a sublime metaphor: the art of skating well. This metaphor sounds the death knell for notions such as "contents" or "secret meanings," in that it acknowledges our life on the surface. Yet, a certain grace, skill, and *savoir vivre* are not only possible but all the more urgent.

E. Emerson's summation is expressed in biblical terms as the Fall of Man.

    1. We are doomed to mediation, to consciousness, to never having direct access to things or others.

    2. Our highest constructs—such as Jesus—change. This is quite a statement from a former minister, and it is easy to see that the Church would not have been comfortable with such views.

    3. Emerson argues that our life is an ongoing series of discoveries, and experience records our crashing into both reality and ourselves. The universe discovers us to ourselves, makes us cognizant of our systems, and gives us our estate.

4. Emerson concludes, much like the Existentialists do, that we are ultimately "unsponsored and free" (in Wallace Stevens' terms), but he goes on to suggest that our "islanded" condition is a creative poverty.

5. Emerson's wisdom is the perfect complement to Voltaire's isolationism: *cultiver son jardin*. Unlike the French philosopher, however, Emerson means that we must "cultivate" our own earth, our own substance.

Readings:

Essential: Emerson: *Nature*, "The American Scholar," "The Poet," "History," "The Oversoul," "Self-Reliance," "Circles," "Experience" in *Essays and Lectures* (New American Library, 1983)

Recommended: Matthiessen, *American Renaissance* (Oxford University Press, 1941); Kazin, *An American Procession* (Vintage, 1985)

Topics for Further Consideration:

1. Explain how Emerson's pronouncements about language in general and American culture in particular forecast developments in 19th-century American literature.

2. Conclude whether Emerson's view of self-reliance simplifies or complicates human behavior. Defend your answer.

Lecture Six—Transcript
Emerson Tomorrow—
Deconstructing Culture and Self

This is Lecture Six. It's the last of my lectures on Emerson. I want predominantly to focus on two of his more obscure, but, I think, more provocative and fascinating essays. One is called "Circles," and then I'll spend most time with his really grand piece called "Experience." In order to preface what is so unusual about these pieces, I want to circle back a little bit and talk about the way Emerson has been understood in the histories of American literature that have been written.

There wasn't much history of American literature in the 19th century, although there was a lot of American literature. It wasn't really thought in the Academy that American literature was something one could really study. In the heyday of beginning to think about American literature as a discipline—which is really in the early years of this century, in the 20th century—we have a particular kind of taste that is reigning. It's that moment of the great modernist, T.S. Eliot, Faulkner—writers of that stamp. What you get is a kind of view of American literature that changes the importance of particular writers.

Everyone had known that Emerson was a very revered figure in the 19th century; but, when people start writing 20th century histories of American literature at that time, he is essentially marginalized. The reason for this is the Modernists' privileged complexity and alienation. This is the moment when Melville is rediscovered, is pulled out of obscurity. This is almost the moment when Emily Dickinson becomes readable. Even a figure like Whitman, who's much more self-evidently central to us than he was to 19th century readers, becomes valued, too. Emerson, who was so central a figure, gets marginalized and gets written off as cheery, optimistic, a kind of dewy-eyed belief in American freedom—American democracy—all of these sorts of slogans. Whereas, you get instead, a view of the great American writer as an alienated countercultural figure writing against society, almost by definition, undiscovered during his or her lifetime. Well, Emerson, obviously, is clearly indicted on that front. He was the most revered intellectual of his time.

The Modernist reading gets it wrong. Emerson, in fact, can be plenty obscure, and in fact, moves, as his title says, "in circles" and is a more provocative, complex author in these two essays that I want to look at than we have thought. He leads to the kind of thinking that we think of as the beginnings of Modernism. We see this in the work of Nietzsche, and we also see it in contemporary thinkers and philosophers like Michele Foucault. About the way in which culture is something that is external, but that moves inside of people and makes up the actual complexity and character of their own subjectivity. If we think of our subjectivity as being ours, that sense of a possessive pronoun is what gets us in trouble. I think Emerson is a very brilliant precursor along these lines.

I'm going to read you from "Circles" a couple of passages. One is, "Our life is an apprenticeship to the truth that around every circle, another can be drawn, that there is no end in nature." What he's really saying is that there are no boundaries and there are no lines. Everything we take to be horizons, contours, whether it's about truths, about values, about the phenomena of nature, the more we learn, the more we realize that they are inscribed in other patterns. That the world is serial, that the world is dialectical, that nothing has the kind of clarity or authority or hegemony that we're accustomed to. He also makes it clear—and this is the point that Foucault and modern writers have emphasized but that no one has thought much to look for Emerson—in this argument, that the coherence of any cultural moment is a strange thing, that it holds, it obtains for a while, and when a certain idea or two stops being believable, the culture dies, and we can't read it anymore. It doesn't make sense anymore. We'd like to think that certain things are timeless or that they're universal. These are very, very popular beliefs, and they're much under fire in modern thinking.

Emerson: "Our culture is the predominance of an idea which draws after it this train of cities and institutions. Let us rise into another idea, and they will disappear." All of our institutions will become incoherent. They won't make any sense if the paradigm—which is Thomas Kuhn's famous word for it—if we have a paradigm shift, and we stop looking at the world the same way. Then we will lose the secret, we'll lose the key, and we'll lose the cogency of other cultures. He gives a bunch of examples. He talks about Greek sculpture. We can't really understand it. We have it. We can admire it. But the secret, the genius of it, is alien to us now. He says the same is true for Greek literature, Greek civilization. They depended on a particular set of informing notions. We call that "discourse." That's the word that Foucault uses for it. That we are all always part of an operative discourse that we can't see but that is the thread that holds together the fabric that we think of as intelligible things.

"Everything looks permanent," he writes, "until its secret is known." What a sad remark. "Everything looks permanent until its secret is known." Then we see how it was constructed, how it held for a moment, did its time, and is now a relic and something of the past. "The key to every man is his thought. Sturdy and defying though he look, he has a helm which he obeys, which is the idea after which all his facts are classified." That there is a governing point that makes things coherent. If you shift that point, they stop cohering. That there's a kind of cancellation and obsolescence can be built into this. "For it is the inert effort of every thought having formed itself into a circular wave of circumstance as, for instance"—and listen to his examples—"an empire, rules of an art, a local usage, a religious rite." The Roman Empire—I'm going to give you examples—writing sonnets, taking tea, the Eucharist. "It forms itself into a circular wave of circumstance to heap itself on that ridge and to solidify and him in the life." What he's saying is that there is a kind of indigenous energy that wants to reify things, wants to take our rituals, our constructs, our notions, and say, "This is reality."

What he is suggesting, in a very bold notion here, is that this fights life. Life is change. Life is evolution. Life metamorphoses. The soul moves. The soul becomes. Instead, we have these structures, these rigidified, reified structures—often they're literally structures of churches and courthouses and things like that—where we want to say, "This is the permanent, enduring universal form of reality and of belief." He says it hems in the life. It becomes sterile. It becomes anti-life, counter-life. There's something remarkably free wheeling about the thought that's expressed in this essay. You remember that first line? "Every circle, we will learn, is circumscribed by still other circles." He's also going to write, "There's no such thing as a wall." There's a very famous poem by Robert Frost called "Mending Wall," where the wall becomes an emblem of a kind of parochial way of thinking.

He says there aren't any walls in nature. There are no walls in reality. All of the demarcations and horizons are only horizons that we post.

They're not out there, in the things themselves. Emerson has no illusions about the amount of havoc that this view will wreak. That this is the cause of war, discord, murder, and imprisonment—is when systems become challenged. Think of religious systems. Think of the cause of the wars that we've known. They become challenged because another group says, "That's no longer viable. We don't believe that anymore." "The new statement," he writes, "is always hated by the old and to those dwelling in the old, comes like an abyss of skepticism." What a wonderful choice of words. We call those people skeptics because they don't believe in what we believe in. They may have another belief system, but we call them skeptics because they have rejected our so-called universal system. This is a view that embraces change because change is part of the operation. People will fight it. They've always fought it. That's the history of the world. He knows this partly because of his own sense of his own mercurial identity. He is kaleidoscopic.

There's a wonderful consonance in Emerson, between his sense of what it's like to be a living person and his philosophy about the world and about reality. "Our moods do not believe in each other." What a great line. "Our moods do not believe in each other." When we're angry, that anger has forgotten that we were happy five minutes earlier.

> Our moods do not believe in each other. To-day I am full of thoughts and can write what I please. I see no reason why I should not have the same thought, the same power of expression to-morrow. What I write, whilst I write it, seems the most natural thing in the world; but yesterday I saw a dreary vacuity in this direction in which now I see so much; and a month [hence], I doubt not, I shall wonder who he was that wrote so many continuous pages.

This is a real sense of our selves as being discontinuous—ebb, flow, no pattern there. That's what life is, ebb, flow, evolution, metamorphoses. Could there be an ethos here? Well, you've already seen it in the essay on self-reliance. The ethos is to rely in this, to trust this, except he's going to express it in a more extreme term—which many of us, I think, would be reluctant to believe in—that is "abandonment." He says, "We have to be surprised out of our propriety." Propriety, in the sense of holding onto ourselves—that self-governance that says, "I am, after all, supposed to represent…"

and then fill in the blank—we have to be surprised out of it. We have to lose our semi-eternal memory. So we have to become amnesiac to become free. Forget about the stranglehold of the things we've done in the past. Do something without knowing how or why, that's what we have to do. In short, draw a new circle. "The way of life is wonderful," and he means "wonderful" in the strong sense of the word, full of wonder. "The way of life is wonderful. It is by abandonment." Abandonment. He doesn't mean getting lost. He means throwing yourself into yourself, following instinct, enthusiasm. That's all from "Circles."

I want now to move to the even more astonishing piece, which is "Experience," which I think is very much indebted to the great final essay by Montaigne the French philosopher of the 16th century whom Emerson revered and about whom Emerson wrote, and whose final essay is also called *"Le Experience,"* "About Experience." There are a lot of parallels between them. This essay, which is titled "Experience," you would expect to begin with a kind of confidant sense that we have experience. Instead, it begins with the view that we live in a dream. "Where do we find ourselves?" This is the first line. "Where do we find ourselves? In a series of which we do not know the extremes and believe that it has none." This is the same imagery that T.S. Eliot's going to use. "We wake and find ourselves on a stair. There are stairs below us, which we seem to have ascended. There are stairs above us, many a one, which go upward and out of sight." Here we are in the midst. We cannot see the horizons. We can't see the future. We can't see the past. We're in the murk.

"Sleep lingers all our lifetime about our eyes." This wrecks any notion of having a confident, clear, lucid picture of things. "As night hovers all day in the bows of the fur tree. All things swim and glitter." There's a wonderful elasticity in this man, a capacity to absolutely be alive to—and accepting of—evanescence, instability, discontinuity, change. Murk? Yes, that's what it's about. Clarity is a fiction. So, there's a ghost-like sense of things at the heart of the enterprise here—evanescence and change. It's not clear that there is a unitary shelf. He gives a very moving example of this. He refers to the death of his own child. He says, "The only thing grief has taught me is to know how shallow it is." And this is extraordinarily honest. "Well, souls never touch their objects." He's talking about human love. "An in-navigable sea washes the silent waves between us and the things we aim at and converse with. Grief, too, will make us idealists." That is to say, to realize that only the world of the mind, our mind, is real.

> In the death of my son, now more than two years ago, I seem to have lost a beautiful estate,—no more. I cannot get it nearer to me. If to-morrow I should be informed of the bankruptcy of my principle debtors, the loss of my property would be a great inconvenience to me, perhaps, for many years; but it would leave me as it found me,—neither better nor worse. So is it with this calamity; it does not touch me; something, which I fancied was a part of me, which could not be torn away without tearing me nor enlarged without enriching me, falls off from me and leaves no scar.

That takes a lot of courage to write that after the death of his son. We know that he was moved and distraught. He can write that, even our most intimate and deepest relations are in some terrible way alien to us. They're not us. The only reality is us—it's inside.

He goes on in this essay to talk about the subjectivism of his time. This is something that is consistent with 19th century thinking in general. It's the thing that is at the heart of a book like *Moby Dick*. Emerson writes (I've already suggested to you that we live in a dream world.) "Life is a train of moods like a string of beads, and as we pass through them, they prove to be many colored lenses which paint the world their own hue." Our moods are the way we see the world and, therefore, they are the world. We forget that that's only our way of seeing. "And each shows only what lies in its focus." Remember this notion of lenses. "Our lenses are the way we come to reality. They're the operation that we perform on the world, but we don't see it." We don't know we're wearing these glasses. It's not just the ideas we believe in. It's our moods, it's our temperament, and it's what the Renaissance people would have called our "humors."

This has to do with how we act on the world, but it's an action—an operation—as I said, that is customarily invisible. Emerson finds remarkable language. He says, "Temperament is the iron wire on which the beads are strung." He gives a lot of examples. If you're in a certain kind of mood, the world will not be the same. You'll walk by certain things that, in a different frame of mind, you would value seeing and they would have changed your sense of life. Listen to this: "Temperament also enters fully into the system of illusions and shuts us into a prison of glass, which we cannot see." That's, those lenses again. He at one point says, "We inhabit a temperament," like we are the creatures, the inhabitants, the prisoners, and the inmates of whatever temperament we have at a particular moment. That is life for us.

Well, how do you solve this one? What solution? What would you tell people to do if this subjective grip is so strong and there can't be a kind of shared objective world out there? Emerson argues that what we need to do is to be all the more active, energetic, impulsive, and, above all, not to waste our time theorizing. This is useful in today's Academy, I think, this advice. He puts it in terms of education. "Life is not dialectics." I wish my colleagues could hear that.

> Life is not dialectics. We, I think, in these times, have had lessons enough of the futility of criticism. Our young people have thought and written much on labor and reform, and for all that they have written, neither the world nor themselves have got on a step. Intellectual tasting of life will not supersede muscular activity. If a man should consider the nicety of the passage of a piece of bread down his throat, he would starve.

In other words, if you just theorized about what it's going to be like, what operations or complex operations have to go into effect before a piece of bread can go into your throat, you're never going to eat.

> At Education-Farm, the noblest theory of life sat on the noblest figures of young men and maidens, quite powerless and melancholy. It would not rake or pitch a ton of hay; it would not rub down a horse; and the men and the maidens left it pale and hungry.

What we need is something vital, something that is invigorating. We need practice, not theory. We need to be embarked in life and not simply to be speculating or forming notions about it.

Now, how does he describe this practice? You remember from the last essay, "abandonment" is the term. "Give yourself over to the rhythms and pulses of existence." Listen to this phrase. "Nature hates peeping." Nature hates peeping—like Peeping Toms? Scientists are voyeurs, you know, they're sneaking around trying to figure out secrets. What does it really mean? What's behind that? What's the secret there? Nature hates peeping, and our mothers speak her very sense—Nature's sense—when they say, "Children, eat your victuals and say no more of it." That's the way to go through life. It's time to eat. Eat. Don't theorize. Don't talk. "Children, eat your victuals and say no more of it. To fill the hour, that is happiness. To fill the hour and leave no crevice for a repentance or an approval." Then hear this remarkable line. "We live amid surfaces and the true art of life is to skate well on them."

Do you realize the whole metaphysics of content, depth, secrets, the secret heart of things is being cashiered? It's being put out of business here. Life is surface. Life is the phenomenal surface world that we inhabit. It's the things we can touch. Let's live there. Let's not forget about that in some pointless futile search for secrets and for meanings. "Depth is a fiction." Here he turns inside out, some of his own earlier notions. You'll recall at the very beginning, when we talked about language, he said that the country people have a kind of "pith" that we have lost in the cities. Here he says, and we would think that they're closer to life. "We fancy that we are strangers and not so intimately domesticated in the planet as the wild man and the wild beast and the bird. But the exclusion reaches them, also, reaches the climbing, flying, gliding, feathered and four-footed man. Fox and woodchuck, hawk and snipe and bittern, when nearly seen, have no more root in a deep world than man, and are just such superficial (in the literal sense, "on the surface") tenets of the globe then the new molecular philosophy shows astronomical interspaces between atom and atom." This was written in the 1830s and 1840s. "And shows that the world is all outside." It has no inside.

Again, our metaphysics of depth, of going to the core of things, this informs our way of dealing with one another. We talk about deep feelings, deep ideas. Superficial is a pejorative term in our culture. He's saying, "No, no. It's the surface and that's all we have. That's what's real and the rest is speculation and it keeps us away from, out of touch with, the surfaces themselves." His final summation is expressed in wonderfully Biblical terms. Hear the humor of this. "It's very unhappy, but too late to be helped, the discovery we made that we exist. That discovery is called the Fall of Man. Ever afterwards, we suspect our instruments. We've learned that we do not see directly, but immediately." All of modern life comes out of that view. We don't see directly, but immediately. We wear lenses. We have blinders. We have frames. That's what this whole essay's been about. We have no direct access. "We do not see directly, but immediately, and that we have no means of correcting these colored and distorting lenses, which we are, or of computing the amount of their errors. Perhaps these subject lenses have a creative power. Perhaps there are no objects."

That's even stranger. The lenses we have don't just distort things, they manufacture the whole world for us. They don't just give us a particular take on them, they're out there engendering the vision itself, all of it. "Once we lived in what we saw." I guess that would have been when we were living in Eden. "Now, the rapaciousness of this new power which threatens to absorb all things engages us." So, there is a fabulous recognition here that we live in mediation. We live at or removed from things. We have these lenses that are between the world and us. What we have are these governing constructs that shape cogency for us. "All things are subject to change. People forget that it is the eye which makes the horizon." The horizon is not there to the eye. We construct it through our lenses, through our engendering vision. He claims that we construct everything we see on it. We construct heroes. We construct saints. "Jesus, the providential man, is a good man on whom many are agreed that these optical laws shall take effect." Christianity is an optical code that says that Jesus is the person who epitomizes providential man. There will be a time when that will fall apart and another code will come about, and this will be as esoteric or exotic to us as religions from tribal cultures that we don't understand anymore.

All is perspective. There's a remarkable wisdom in much of this. There's a sense here that we are cut off, and yet there's no "blue funk" in this essay. There's no sense that this is a kind of prison of relativity, which is how we would tend to think of it today. Emerson is going to argue over and over that this is a source of freedom. Here is a line of Emerson's thought that goes, not only to figures like Nietzsche—that we are unsponsored—the death of God is one of things he's talking about—but also it will go on, as I said, to Foucault. It will go into the poets like Wallace Stevens. His term is that we are "unsponsored," and, therefore, free.

There is a wonderful sense here in which self-reliance comes back into the picture. It is true that this "self" no longer has quite the credentials that it had in the earlier essays, and yet it is all we ever will have. That's why I say there's no sense of a blue funk here. This is a creative condition to be in. It's one that frees us. "It is true that all the muses and love and religion hate these developments," he says. "And will find a way to punish the chemist who publishes in the parlor the secrets of the laboratory. We cannot say too little of our constitutional necessity of seeing things under private aspects or saturated with our humors." But he adds, "And yet, is God the native of these bleak rocks?" It's a line that Wallace could have written. "And yet, is God the native of these bleak rocks?" This is our landscape. This is our self. It is true we exist in mediation to the world, that we skate on the surface. Yet, those bleak rocks, that's the divinity that we have. It's not in some esoteric code anywhere. There's cause for celebration. "We must hold hard to this poverty, however scandalous. And by more vigorous self recoveries after the sallies of action, possess our axis ever more firmly."

Self-possession is really the project. That's the goal. He ends up expressing it in language that reminds me a lot of his predecessor, Voltaire, whose most famous phrase is, *"Il faut cultiver son jardin"* "One must cultivate one's garden." That is a kind of pragmatism that Voltaire puts forth as, "Stay away from metaphysics, stay away from philosophy; stick to the here and now, and to the basics." Here's how Emerson closes—you'll see that he turns a twist on this. "We dress our garden, eat our dinners, discuss the household with our wives, and these things make no impression and are forgotten next week." These are the routine habits of a life. They're not part of us. They don't gut in deep. "But, in the solitude to which every man is always returning, he has his sanity and revelations which, in his passage into new worlds, he will carry with him." You return to your solitude, mediated though your relation to the world is. Those are your riches. It's a bare landscape, but it is the only divinity that you will know. It is where God lives. It's the place of God.

I said he is modeling this essay after Montaigne. Montaigne gives us the term, he calls it the *"arriere-boutique,"* the shop in the back of the shop. He uses that as a metaphor for the human soul that we all retire in some fashion to this back shop for our deepest transactions. I think Emerson is being 100 percent loyal here to Montaigne. Except, that this back shop, for Montaigne, has become the only shop. For Emerson, it is the full stage, but it's a huge stage. It's the inner resources of the self where we have to finally take root and find divinity.

Lecture Seven
Henry David Thoreau—Countercultural Hero

Scope:

Seen initially as eccentric and derivative, both Thoreau and his masterpiece, *Walden*, have undergone drastic reevaluations over time. Thoreau has been viewed as moralist, environmentalist, political philosopher, and guru. Beginning with an overview of Thoreau's successive "images," we will focus our investigation on *Walden*, with an eye toward its special appeal to the young. Thoreau's views on personal freedom lead him to the conviction that civilized life, with its rampant materialism, constitutes an absurd prison. Thoreau goes to the woods to encounter reality in its elemental form, and in so doing he establishes a kind of quintessential American dream that lurks behind (or beyond) the writings and the lives of countless Americans. Yet Thoreau is no less fascinating as stylist than as moralist, and his pithy metaphors and aphorisms are now part of our everyday language. Ultimately *Walden* intrigues us today as a meditation on our rich, sometimes tragic, relationship to nature, a relationship highlighted by contemporary thinking about the environment. The life of *Walden*, a piece of literature forever fresh, is inevitably to be contrasted with the life of Walden Pond, an at-risk tourist spot in Massachusetts.

Thoreau's contemporaries regarded him as a shadow to Emerson, and his philosophy of "self-reliance" and American promise does resemble that of Emerson, who was his mentor. But, unlike Emerson, Thoreau also stands tall in the history of political dissent, and perhaps taller still as champion of the environment. In *Walden*, he gives us not only the poem of the earth, but also the still more seductive poem of our "home" in the woods: an ecstatic opportunity to discover reality, that of nature and of the self. It is enough, Thoreau says, to "know beans," thereby suggesting how ephemeral and superficial our ordinary projects are. This homespun pragmatism, a coming-to-terms with the basics, is what ultimately seduces in *Walden*; it remains eternally appealing in a society that has lost its contact with the land.

Objectives: Upon completion of this lecture, you should be able to:

1. Explain how Thoreau's political views were reflected in the nature of his literary undertakings.

2. Compare and contrast the Thoreauvian and Emersonian conceptions of the individual.

3. Summarize why *Walden* represents the quintessential American experiment.

Outline

I. Thoreau's career is something of a roller-coaster affair. His contemporaries did not take him seriously, but rather dismissed him as something of a quack at worst, or Emerson's acolyte at best.

    A. The charge that Thoreau was Emerson's follower has much truth; Emerson allowed Thoreau to live on his land at Walden Pond. Emerson's stirring orations about American promise and democracy are central to Thoreau's work.

    B. Thoreau is also, however, to be understood as one of the seminal political dissenters in American culture.

        1. In 1846, Thoreau refused to pay several years' poll tax, in protest against Massachusetts' role in perpetuating slavery; he spent one night in jail.

        2. Thoreau published "Civil Disobedience" in 1848, a relatively unnoticed text at the time, but one that later proved to be of enormous significance in its impact on figures such as Gandhi and Martin Luther King.

        3. In 1851, enraged by passage of the Fugitive Slave Act, Thoreau again became active in the abolitionist movement and was said to be involved with the Underground Railroad.

        4. In 1859, after the fateful raid on Harper's Ferry carried out by John Brown, Thoreau read publicly "A Plea for Captain John Brown," one of his most passionate political speeches, just days before Brown's execution.

    C. Thoreau is perhaps most compelling to us in the late 20th century as the environmentalist of the 19th century.

        1. Consider the environmental undertones of his titles: "A Week on the Concord and Merrimack Rivers,"

"Walden," "On Life In The Woods," "The Maine Woods," "Cape Cod."

2. With 150 years of distance between Thoreau's writing and our analysis, and with a now-established tradition of nature writing from Rachel Carson to Peter Matthiessen and John McPhee, Thoreau can be seen as the beginning of a tradition, and his light shines brightly.

3. Walden (1854) is Thoreau's masterpiece, and although the work is not explicitly political, we cannot miss its message about the stewardship of nature.

II. Thoreau has proven to be a guru for the young, and it is not hard to see why his message strikes a chord in the rising generation, especially in our time.

A. Thoreau's put-down of the elders is very pronounced; steeped though he is in classical learning, he defiantly claims that the "fathers" of his society have nothing to teach him.

B. Thoreau, more than Emerson, elects to *live out* his principles by moving to Walden Pond; hence, he articulates a philosophy of action, of praxis over theory.

C. The cornerstone of Thoreau's vision is that we are all entrapped by the prison-house of culture, and he illustrates this concept in striking ways.

1. We are all slaves in society, according to Thoreau, in that we follow routines and even worship gods that are patently artificial, conventional, and unrelated to our own true needs.

2. To buttress his views, Thoreau urges us to grasp the basic concepts of economics that undergird every act of our lives; in short, he redefines the true "cost of living" as the amount of "life" that we pay for whatever we do.

3. "The mass of men lead lives of quiet desperation" is one of Thoreau's famous remarks. It goes well beyond recognition of habit and routine to imply a neurosis of everyday life, a frightening sense that we are all suffering a living death.

4. Marching to a different drummer is Thoreau's explanation for all those who would be themselves, who would jettison the herd mentality.

5. Much like Emerson, Thoreau developed a pungent antisocial philosophy, making it clear that we are essentially wasting our time and ourselves when we are involved in society.

6. Why do charity? Thoreau does not hesitate to attack this shibboleth of polite 19th-century thinking, suggesting that he is not personally cut out for such work; hence it is to be rejected.

7. It follows from Thoreau's cavalier view of society that he is equally committed to getting clear of the State as well; here, too, we see a potent strand of thinking in the American weave.

8. Thoreau's program is draconian: avoid all commitment. We need to determine at what point this ideal of freedom may conceal a monstrous egoism.

D. *Walden*, the enduring work of Thoreau, is our quintessential American experiment, destined to have a long life in the aspirations of our nation.

1. Living alone in the woods, Thoreau decides to encounter reality at last, to get clear of all distractions and abstractions, to get to the pith of experience.

2. Knowing beans may seem trivial to an industrialized society, but Thoreau makes us understand its grandeur: to at last have authentic knowledge.

3. Many of Thoreau's most engaging passages have to do with developing the inner man. This argument is appropriately expressed in terms of rejecting ornament and clothing.

4. Speaking a great deal in metaphors of ownership and property, Thoreau constantly juxtaposes the material with the spiritual. His goal consists of possessing one's "real" estate: earth and sky. No mortgage or price tag is involved.

Lecture Seven—Transcript
Henry David Thoreau—Countercultural Hero

This is Lecture Seven, and it's the first of three lectures that I'm going to give on Thoreau. Thoreau, of course, is a canonical figure in American 19th century letters. He's our Rousseau, the man who left society and lived in the woods. He's the first great environmentalist. He's a political radical. He could have invented the term, "Small is better." He's also a kind of Yankee poet-aphorist, with a tone and a kind of smack in his language that is unforgettable. Some people have said that he writes too cutely, that his writing is almost overdone. One of the lectures that I'm going to give will have to do with his style. I want to start with Thoreau, the countercultural figure, and then focus in the second lecture on his style, and then close, obviously, with *Walden*—although *Walden* will be the substance of all of my remarks—but close with *Walden* in a kind of double way. About what it means to celebrate a particular pond that is threatened by the forces, that nature is threatened by today, and what it means to create a work of art that remains fresh and that is not subject to spoil.

I'll talk more about this in a later lecture, but I'll mention it now. Thoreau is a modern figure in the sense that the 19th century did not pay attention to him, at least not as a major writer. He was thought to be a kook, quirky, an Emerson follower—an acolyte. I think that there are lines that I enjoy in Thoreau that sound a lot like Emerson. For example, he, like Emerson, champions America. There's a kind of patriotism there, about getting clear of Europe, getting clear of a kind of past tradition that has nothing to do with what's indigenous in America. "Some are dinning in our ears that we Americans, and moderns in general, are intellectual dwarfs compared with the ancients or even the Elizabethan men. Well, what is that to the purpose? A living dog is better than a dead lion." Emerson probably would not have written that last line, "A living dog is better than a dead lion." There's a kind of zip and a kind of causticness in Thoreau where you begin to get something of his flavor.

Here's another one about the virtues of being a democratic self as opposed to, let's say, a figure in a class society. "I would rather sit on a pumpkin and have it all to myself than to be crowded on a velvet cushion. I would rather ride on earth in an oxcart with a free circulation than go to heaven in the fancy car of an excursion train and breathe a malaria all the way." He's a little xenophobic, I think. I mean, there's a real sense here that we've got the goods right here in Massachusetts. That's what counts. That's the right life. This is a necessary kind of utterance in mid-century. He is known today in a way that he wasn't then, as the great father of political dissent.

There's a story there that's worth rehearsing for you a little bit. In 1846, Thoreau refused to pay several years of poll taxes—back taxes—and it was a protest against Massachusetts' role in perpetuating slavery. He was very fervently anti-slavery. So he was arrested, and spent one night in jail. Somebody else paid the fine. This was not much talked about at that point. He later writes a text that we now call *Civil Disobedience*. It too was not much talked about at the time. He wrote it in 1848, and it has become a classic. Why? Not because of the Academy, but because it was a key strategic text for Ghandi, for Martin Luther King, and for other people who have stood up to the oppressiveness of the State and made the argument for individual freedom. Thoreau has acquired a kind of eminence and stature, and a kind of political identity that no one thought to give him in the same way in the 19th century. I don't want to overstate this because he was politically involved.

In 1851, for example, he was enraged—as was Harriet Beecher Stowe—by the passage of the Fugitive Slave Act, which meant that slaves captured or found—even in the north—one was legally required to send them back to the south. It is said that he—this is arguable—but, it's said that he was involved with the Underground Railroad for escaping slaves to get out of the south. He's been alleged to have sheltered escaped slaves in his own—course he didn't have much of a house—but nonetheless, to put them up—to keep them. He was particularly incensed with what happened to John Brown. You know that the story of John Brown's organized raid on Harper's Ferry is argued by some people to be the cause of the Civil War. Brown was arrested, and Brown was executed. Shortly before the execution, Thoreau wrote one of his most passionate political speeches called "A Plea for Captain John Brown." He went around New England reading this speech with great fervor and emotion. He read it in Concord, obviously, but he read it in Boston, he read it in Worcester. There is a kind of interesting political history there that, in a sense for many, looms larger than anything else in his work.

He's also a great environmentalist, as I said. Listen to the titles, "A Week on the Concord and Merrimac Rivers," *Walden* or its subtitle "On Life in the Woods," "The Maine Woods," "Cape Cod." Every single thing he wrote is about a natural preserve or his experience in nature. Environmentalism was not a term that existed in the 19th century. So here too, just as his political reputation is in some sense the creation of a later age, so too is his reputation and stature as a man who was interested in the stewardship of the environment. I think that's a very serious claim for his eminence.

Moreover, we can read his work differently because we have a tradition, let's say it goes back at least to Rachel Carson, *Silent Spring*. But then writers like Peter Matthiessen, John McPhee, are nature writers who help us to return to Thoreau and see him as the origin—in some ways—of an entire discourse about nature. Still, no one would argue about the claim that *Walden* is his masterpiece. It in a sense contains the entire agenda—of all the things that I've talked about—in its brightest form. There is a lot of righteous indignation about the abuse of the land. I'll read you one particularly scathing remark. He has gone to this pond that's called Flint's Pond. As you know, ponds are named after the farmers who live in that area.

> Flint's Pond! Such is the poverty of our nomenclature. What right had the unclean and stupid farmer, whose farm abutted on this sky water, whose shores he has ruthlessly laid bare, to give his name to it? Some skin-flint, who loved better the reflecting surface of a dollar, or a bright cent, in which he could see his own brazen face; who regarded even the wild ducks which settled in it as trespassers; his fingers grown into crooked and bony talons from the long habit of grasping harpy-like; —so it is not named for me. I go not there to see him nor to hear of him; who never saw it, who never bathed in it, who never loved it, who never protected it, who never spoke a good word for it, nor thanked God that He had made it.

That's pretty strong stuff. You don't own nature but you are to revere nature. Nature is the handiwork of the Lord and, that by this type of ownership—which as you are going to see is a very great sore spot in Thoreau's philosophy—that we are shackled. He's going to claim by our possessions—and particularly odious is the claim— that we could own or possess nature.

Now this man, predictably, like Emerson, has a philosophy of action. I think what I've just told you about his curriculum vitae bears that out. Emerson was never a political radical. Emerson also was incensed about what happened to John Brown. Emerson was also an abolitionist—but never activist in the way that Thoreau was. In fact, there's probably an apocryphal statement that when Emerson when to visit Thoreau in jail, he said, "what are you doing here, Henry?" And Thoreau's answer was, "You should be here." That's one of the operative distinctions between these two figures, that Emerson didn't quite promote the same kind of vigorous enactment in your everyday life in the social and political gestures. "To be a philosopher is not merely to have subtle thoughts, nor even to found a school, but so to love wisdom as to live according to its dictates a life of simplicity, independence, magnanimity, and trust."

Now Thoreau, much more than Emerson, appeals to the young. There's something endearing and heartwarming when you're a student and young, trying to make your own way, to read Thoreau because he has such impudence about the authority of the Fathers. He's willing to tell you straight out that he never learned anything from anybody old.

> Practically, the old have no very important advice to give to the young, their own experience has been so partial, and their lives have been such miserable failures, for private reasons, as they must believe; and it may be that they have some faith left which belies that experience, and they are only less young than they were. I've lived some thirty years on this planet, and I have yet to hear the first syllable of valuable or even earnest advice from my seniors. They have told me nothing, and probably cannot tell me anything to the purpose.

I think young people enjoy reading something like that—doesn't make it easy, when you're old, to be telling them to read it though. He also has the same caustic view of the apparent great progress in America that is a theme song in the mid-19th century. We're talking about Jacksonian America. "We are in great haste to construct a magnetic telegraph from Maine to Texas, but Maine and Texas, it may be, have nothing important to communicate." So this is the kind of laconic wit. He also I think really draws a bead on our obsession with being informed about the news.

Hardly a man takes a half-hour's nap after dinner, but when he wakes up he holds up his head and asks, 'What's the news?' as if the rest of mankind had stood his sentinels. Some give directions to be waked every half-hour, doubtless for no other purpose; and then to pay for it, they tell what they have dreamed. After a night's sleep the news is as indispensable as the breakfast. 'Pray tell me anything new that has happened to a man anywhere on this globe'—and he reads it over his coffee and rolls, that a man has had his eyes gouged out this morning on the Wachito River; never dreaming the while that he lives in the dark unfathomed mammoth cave of this world, and has but the rudiment of an eye himself.

So there's a real sense here of our distractedness—and this is Emersonian too—our failure to be attentive to ourselves, to the core of things. We palm this off as being informed, being educated, being concerned. You're going to see that the egoism of Thoreau is, if anything, more extreme, more monstrous even than Emerson. There's really something quite exciting about that. "We are all slaves," according to Thoreau. This is a man who was a real abolitionist. Yet he still says that the Negro slavery is not the worst of it. "There's so many keen and subtle masters that enslave both north and south. It is hard to have a southern overseer. It's worse to have a northern one, but worst of all when you are the slave driver of yourself." So he uses it as a kind of trope metaphor to characterize our general condition.

His project is about emancipation—as is Emerson's—and he expresses it in wonderfully laconic, and in some cases businesslike, terms. Here's one of the most remarkable definitions that I've ever read of how life is business, how we're always transacting business. "How do we measure the cost of things?" You know, we have our phrase, "the cost of living." Usually, people can put a dollar index of it. Not Thoreau. "The cost of a thing is the amount of what I will call life which is required to be exchanged for it, immediately or in the long run." That is a very severe standard. What have we paid to do what we do, to be who we are? Do we measure costs in this existential way that Thoreau is talking about? This is what the real cost of living is, the tradeoffs that we make. This is going to be a massive indictment of the kind of material lures that have pulled us off-track.

One of Thoreau's most famous phrases, "The mass of men lead lives of quiet desperation." There is a wonderful sense that we are not only trapped by our lives but that we're seething, that we're also about to erupt. There's something manic in that phrase, "quiet desperation." Thoreau's work tells you a lot about pent up violence, it seems to me. We all live counterfeit lives in some way. Thoreau is the one who has the very famous line as well about the individual as "a person who marches to a different drummer." "If a man does not keep pace with his companions, perhaps it is because he hears a different drummer." These lines have gone into the language. Thoreau has articulated notions about selfhood, about individuality, that all of us have taken as mother's milk in this country.

Well, like Emerson, Thoreau has an exceedingly sharp, and I think vicious view of society. Who needs it? It's just in the way. I think more even than Emerson, there is something antisocial in Thoreau. That's why Rousseau is an appropriate model here, because there's something of really misanthropic bent in this man. "I find it wholesome to be alone the greater part of the time. To be in company even with the best is soon wearisome and dissipating. I love to be alone. I never found the companion that was so companionable as solitude." Took him four sentences to say the same thing. "Society is commonly too cheap. We meet at very short intervals, not having had time to acquire any new value for each other. We meet at three meals a day, three times a day, and give each other a new taste of that old musty cheese that we are." He doesn't particularly like folks.

He, in one of his chapters, which is called "Visitors," he talks about coming up to people and meeting them and finding how, you know, how strange they look. This is the village, actually. "As I walked in the woods to see the birds and squirrels, so I walked in the village to see the men and boys." Notice the parallel, just a kind of botanical curiosity really.

> …Instead of the wind among the pines, I heard the carts rattle. In one direction from my house there was a colony of muskrats in the river meadows; under the grove of elms and buttonwoods in the other horizon was a village of busy men, as curious to me as if they had been prairie-dogs, each sitting at the mouth of its burrow, or running over to a neighbor's to gossip. I went there frequently to observe their habits.

Like the scientist who's looking in his laboratory at human beings, human beings seemed very strange to Thoreau, like another species. What do you think Thoreau looked like to people? There's a comment from one of his contemporaries. "The Concord people did not understand Emerson or Thoreau or wish to even. The people did not know whether Emerson and Thoreau were fluid or solid, neither did they care." So that you reap what you sow in some sense. But there's almost a sense of pseudo-speciation here, that people aren't really part of the main picture here. So you can imagine not much generosity here, in terms of grand social gestures. Charity for example: "You must have a genius for charity as well as for anything else. As for doing good, that's one of the professions which are full," as if to say, "No need. You can't get a job there. Everybody's done it already." "Moreover, I have tried it fairly, and strange as it may seem, (it's not strange at all,) strange as it may seem, I am satisfied that it does not agree with my constitution." There is just this kind of serene acceptance and complacency that, "I've tried it, didn't feel right, not going to try it again."

So as well, the State—what do you want of the State? The State's just nothing but a troublemaker—gets in your way.

> One afternoon, near the end of first summer, when I went to the village to get a shoe from the cobbler's, I was seized and put into jail, because, as I have elsewhere related, I did not pay a tax to, or recognize the authority of, the State which buys and sells men, women, and children, like cattle, at the door of its senate-house. I had gone to the woods for other purposes. But, wherever a man goes, men will pursue and paw him with their dirty institutions, (Get this language) and, if they can, constrain him to belong to their desperate odd-fellow society.

Dirty institutions. Desperate, odd fellow society. Get out of there, avoid the great term of the recent era—avoid commitment. "But I would say to my fellows once and for all, as long as possible, live free and uncommitted. It makes but little difference whether you're committed to a farm or the county jail." Stay away.

What you have in *Walden* is the fundamental project of getting clear, getting free, of society, of charity, of others, of the State, and having the great American rendezvous, which is nature, life at the core, at its pith, to finally embrace reality. No one has ever written more beautifully than Thoreau about that. "I went to the woods," he writes, "because I wished to live deliberately, to front only the essential facts of life and see if I could not learn what it had to teach and not, when I came to die, discover that I had not lived. I did not wish to live what was not life. Living is so dear." Here comes that business equation again—the cost of it is so great. "Nor did I wish to practice resignation, unless it was quite necessary. I wanted to live deep and suck out all the marrow of life." It's a wonderful image. As I said, these images, this project, has entered into the collective psyche of the United States, certainly of its writers. What is Hemingway if it's not what I'm reading you here? To live in the woods, to have this encounter with nature, to suck out the marrow of life, not to be old and dying and to discover that you have not lived.

"To live so sturdily and Spartan-like as to put to route all that was not life, to cut a broad swath and shave close." Do you hear these wonderful metaphors? He's not talking abstractions. He's putting it constantly in physical, carnal terms, "sucking at the marrow." "To drive life into a corner and reduce it to its lowest terms. And if it prove to be mean, why then to get to the whole and genuine meanness of it and publish its meanness to the world. Or it were sublime, to know it by experience and be able to give a true account of it in my next excursion." As I said, this is the great American rendezvous. This is absolutely, it seems to me, a seminal moment in American thinking and in American values. Much more than Emerson here, Thoreau lived it. He spent a year in the Walden woods.

You can't understand the American '60s; but you can understand, it seems to me, even a book like *Moby Dick*—Ishmael going out to sea. You can understand the American restlessness, particularly among males, to encounter reality at its pith, to face the elements. Of course, there are enormous ramifications and implications in this. It usually means leaving family, leaving society. It frequently is solipsistic. It often entails the rejection of human relationships, of even acknowledging that there are other responsibilities than your own commitment to yourself. This is the logical but brutal consequence of Emersonian individualism. Thoreau, I think, carries it to its appropriate culminating phase.

I hope you can sense that there's something quite beautiful and haunting and seductive here—and pure—but also to be aware of the price that must be paid. And perhaps you can sense the puerile dimension of this because, as we look at later texts—and one has even seen it in earlier texts—I think *Rip Van Winkle* certainly points to this—that there is something escapist perhaps as well in this. So that, what looks on the one hand like a kind of philosophical encounter with truth could also be seen as a fear of—or inability to accept—social, emotional, sexual responsibilities, connections, relations. Thoreau, as I said, is rhapsodic when he talks about this encounter, this effort to get free of culture. I mentioned Hemingway. You could mention Norman Mailer. There are lots and lots of American writers, particularly men, where you have this same effort to confront things in their pith. To get clear of culture is really what it's all about, all of these constraints which appear to be artificial and imprisoning.

His language is poetic language, not because it rhymes, but because it's so muscular. There's something so vivid. For example, "Let us settle ourselves and work and wedge our feet downward through the mud and slush of opinion." Notice the way that metaphor works. You've got your feet there, and you're trying to get through to bedrock, through the mud and slush of opinion and prejudice and tradition and delusion and appearance, that alluvium which covers the globe. It's like the globe is under a crust of mud. We've got to go through it. Through Paris and London, through New York and Boston and Concord, through Church and State. They all participate in this muck that prevents us from getting to truth. Through poetry and philosophy and religion, we have to get our feet through all of that, until we come to a hard bottom and rocks in place, which we can call reality and say, this "is." Make no mistake—be it life or death—we crave only reality. "If we really are dying, let us hear the rattle in our throats and feel cold in the extremities. If we are alive, let us go about our business."

There is, as I said, the rhapsodic Thoreau, but also the poetic Thoreau, who brilliantly exploits this metaphor of going through muck, slush, going through all of those buffers, all of those layers, that culture, tradition, society, and institutions, have constructed between us and bedrock. He's going to locate that at Walden Pond. That's the business of living. There, the transaction you make is worthwhile. The amount of life that you have to pay, there pays off. You get a reward. You get through. As I say, what's most striking is the way in which that is expressed, the reality quest there, to go through convention.

There is a persistent rejection of ornament in Thoreau. Sometimes it's quite funny. He senses that we are always clothed too much in strange fashions, out of touch with what's real, thinking that the external façade is who we are. "I say beware of all enterprises that require new clothes and not rather a new wearer of clothes. We don garment after garment as if we grew like exogenous plants by addition without." Whereas, what he's saying is, what is real is within, behind this layering of social façade. His book is about being fully human, and, like Emerson, coming into one's estate. Like Emerson, he makes the same critique of our habits, of our division of labor.

> Lo! men have become the tools of their tools. The man who independently plucked the fruits when he was hungry is become a farmer; (He did it before when he was hungry. He had a vital relation to the earth. Now it's become his métier, his profession.) and he who stood under a tree for shelter, a housekeeper (kept by the house). We no longer camp as for a night, but have settled down on earth and forgotten heaven.

What a lovely line, "settled down on earth and forgotten heaven." We have become so benighted, by routine, by habit, by job, that we have forgotten that we inhabit a very large place. Walden Pond would seem to be a small place. Concord would seem to be a small place. Only if you think that you are settling down on earth, all you have to do is raise your sights, and you see heaven. So, I want you to think of Thoreau going both directions, down to bedrock, up to heaven.

Lecture Eight
Thoreau—Stylist and Humorist Extraordinaire

Scope:

Much of Thoreau's authority and charm comes from his use of the first person. More than most writers, he cultivated a particular, idiosyncratic style, rich in axioms and unforgettable one-liners, leaving a distinct "flavor" to all his musings. Moreover, there is throughout his life an almost desperate desire to transcribe experience into language, as is evidenced by the massive journals he left, in which he set out to record the experiences of his life. Although there is a twinkle and a wink in much of his work, Thoreau is often misconstrued as humorless and sermonizing.. He deserves more serious accounting as a *writer*, as a 19th-century stubborn Yankee voice that insists on its rights and articulates its homespun idioms. Most memorable are the pungent humor of *Walden* (Thoreau can be brutally satirical) and the splendid evocations of the natural world—at times lyrical, at times mock epic, and often sublime. It is here that Emerson's view of "fact" becoming "spirit" is enacted in front of our eyes.

Objectives: Upon completion of this lecture, you should be able to:

1. Give examples of the mock epic in *Walden*.

2. Explain Thoreau's idea of the relationship between the individual and society.

3. Identify various ways in which Thoreau reveals himself to be a man of business.

Outline

I. *Walden* is written in the first person, and it is an unusual first-person at that, full of idiosyncrasies, willing to underscore its biases.

   A. A question that many first-person texts never answer is "Why say 'I'"? Thoreau, however, is wonderfully up-front here.

      1. Thoreau's first line of defense is his best one: What else do we know, other than "I"?

2. Thoreau also goes on to argue that his touting of his own experience is more public than it appears. He is conducting an experiment for mankind, and hence he is a generic boaster about the promise of life.

B. *Walden* offers an adventure in self-portraiture with a vengeance in that Thoreau is eager to accentuate his oddness, to deliver himself to us—warts and all.

1. Thoreau, in going to the woods, discovers the savage in himself, the man who repudiates all the laws of Boston and Concord, who discovers common ground with the beasts and the elements.

2. Despite his acknowledgment of a certain "wildness," Thoreau ultimately emerges as the ascetic, the man who wants to strip down to bare essentials, who finds it easier to do without than to desire.

3. Thoreau is perhaps our first famous vegetarian; he offers an entire program against the grossness of carnal life, especially when it comes to consuming animal flesh.

II. Thoreau's unforgettable style is what stays with us perhaps the longest.

A. A satirical, pungent writer, he is the unrivaled master of great one-liners, phrases that stick in the imagination once we have read them.

1. Thoreau's remark "The mass of men lead lives of quiet desperation" is one of the great American knife-like utterances about the manic darkness underneath the public discourse of cheery optimism.

2. "I have traveled a good deal in Concord" is the virtual theme song of *Walden*, and once we stop smiling at its quaintness— Concord is very small—we begin to realize how serious this utterance is. Thoreau's text is precisely about the dimensionality of Walden Pond, the huge universes that one charts by spending a year in the woods.

3. Thoreau's remark, "If a man does not keep pace with his companions, perhaps it is because he hears a different drummer" is the cardinal principle of American individualism and nonconformity.

B. Thoreau is, above all, one of the great humorists of his age.

1. One of Thoreau's most telling metaphors about authenticity and the need to get clear of social convention revolves around the "clothing" of the age.
2. Thoreau deliciously recounts his grand adventure at Walden Pond in the most pragmatic terms: he is the consummate businessman, doing his "job" in the best place possible.
3. Thoreau's coolness and antisocial attitudes show up in his frequent dilemma: how to suffer fools? He disposes of them with dispatch.
4. "Running risks" is a time-honored metaphor for the dangerous and authentic life; Thoreau the adventurer rings a change on the idiom.
5. Thoreau's sassiness, his insolence vis-à-vis conventional polite values, is nowhere more visible than in his commentary on common sense.

C. The poetry of *Walden* is what we most remember. It is here that Emerson's injunctions about the right kind of new language make most sense.

1. From earth to heaven is the classic directionality of *Walden*; this text that seems so earth-bound makes transcendental moves over and over.
2. From matter to spirit is the guiding principle of Thoreau's vision and style. Again and again he shocks us by revealing the reach of his subject, by showing us that a description of "things" is merely a lead-in to an account of the soul.
3. At his best, Thoreau is writing about claiming our estate, and in one of his most splendid metaphors, he inverts water and sky; making us realize that we are drinking heaven.
4. *Walden* has many set, rhetorical themes, but Thoreau's brilliance is also to be found in his casual references, his throwaway, organic style that rules everywhere.

5. One of Thoreau's most noted effects in *Walden* is his use of mock epic, the invocation of Homeric figures and epithets to describe mosquitoes and ants. This is more than just a satirical account; it's a demonstration of wonders.

6. "Re-peopling" the woods is one of Thoreau's singular phrases, and this metaphor causes us to reconceive his apparently solipsistic existence in the woods.

7. Thoreau's ongoing comparisons with natural creatures evoke a new kind of poetry—birds sing as they work. We realize that there is a genuine symbiosis among living/working/singing and that Thoreau's text is out to demonstrate such a model.

8. Thoreau's bottom line seems to be: the song of the earth is the song of the heavens. That is, if we can perceive the first, then we are well on to the path of encountering the second.

Lecture Eight—Transcript
Thoreau—Stylist and Humorist Extraordinaire

This is Lecture Eight, and it's my second lecture on Thoreau. I'd like to focus this lecture on Thoreau as a stylist, but also Thoreau as a humorist. Let me spell out a little bit what I have in mind here. Stylist, for many people, sounds like a kind of frill notion, like "we want the ideas not the style." I think the ideas in Thoreau often are the style. That this is more than a question of verbal ornamentation or particular tropes or choices that he makes. It's more than just a kind of language. It's a vision; and, it's a view of language that is very much indebted to Emerson—leading to a view of the world. You remember Emerson's semiotics, that words are signs of spirit, that nature is signs of spirit. I think that Thoreau is one of the most splendid exemplars of this, so that it's a style that we need to attend to. We really want to understand what Thoreau is doing, even if we don't attend to it. I think it inevitably is part of why we like this text—if we like it.

Humorist. Most people don't think of Thoreau as particularly humorous, that he seems to be in the eyes of many a kind of stodgy humorless sermonizing character who tells us how nice he had it in the woods. I think it's important to rescue him from that, to realize that he has a kind of wacky, goofy sense of humor at times, that there's really something irrepressible about him. Maybe it's a feature of his contempt for people that this absolutely frees up the tongue as well. But since this is a literature course, and since I love to read text aloud, I think we should try to have a little fun with this figure as well. So I want to talk about his unusual highlighting of himself, of the first person. He says it in the very first page of *Walden*. He draws our attention to it.

"In most books, the I, or first person, is omitted." He's thinking of books of science, books of history, information. "In this, it will be retained. That, in respect to egotism, is the main difference. We commonly do not remember that it is after all always the first person that is speaking. I should not talk so much about myself if there were anybody else whom I knew as well." What a fine, fine confession, that this is the unstated truth of all texts, even the most rigorously scientific and impersonal and objective, that they too must stem from someone's experience. We can't write "we." We can write it all the time, W-E, but we can't be "we." We are always "I." So I think that

Thoreau on the one hand is covering a very important base there that's a kind of honesty.

He'll refer back to this. At times, he will try to speak for him as a kind of exemplary figure. There's a very well known remark that he is bragging, and he's worried that he's going to be thought of as a braggart, and he says, "my boasting is about mankind, it's not about me." It's not my personal life that I'm trying to celebrate. It's rather my experience, which could be exemplary, that others could also have, and it's about the potential and possibilities of everyone's life. So he's thought a lot about where he is in this text as a speaker and how we might or might not respond to that voice. There's a lot of self-portraiture in Thoreau, in *Walden*. He speaks of the savagery that he has uncovered within himself. "I found in myself, and still find, an instinct toward a higher, or as it is named, 'spiritual life,' as do most men, and another toward a primitive, rank, and savage one. I reverence them both." That's an interesting line. Whitman was going to do something very similar. "I reverence them both. I love the wild not less than the good."

I think if you're looking for a wild man, however, in *Walden*, you can often be disappointed. What seems to emerge more than anything else is the aestheticism. There's something almost monastic about a lot of *Walden*. In particular, monastic and aesthetic in ways that are very contemporary with our own time, with our terrible—I think—over-concern about eating right, drinking right, living right, jogging—all of these strategies that presumably will make us eternal. Thoreau buys into a lot of that. He could be popular again today. Much of *Walden* could be on t-shirts. He really fits in with a kind of politically correct society, about slogans that you will do-or-die for. For example, he is against—he's one of the earliest vegetarians. "The gross feeder is a man in the larvae state, and there are whole nations in that condition, nations without fancy or imagination, whose vast abdomens betray them. However, have no fear." He's confident that this will gradually get wiped out.

> Whatever my own practice may be, I have no doubt that it is a part of the destiny of the human race, in its gradual improvement, to leave off eating animals, as surely as the savage tribes have left off eating each other when they came in contact with the more civilized.

Now, where do you end up if you stop eating animal flesh? Well, today we'd say, well, you go into veggies and things like that. Why stop there? Thoreau wants to go much further.

> I believe that water is the only drink for a wise man; wine is not so noble a liquor; and think of dashing the hopes of a morning with a cup of warm coffee, or of an evening with a dish of tea! Ooh, how low I fall when I am tempted by them! Even music may be intoxicating. (Get this? Like music could corrupt you, spoil you.) Such apparently slight causes destroyed Greece and Rome, and will destroy England and America. Of all ebriosity, (of all drunkenness) who does not prefer to be intoxicated by the air he breathes?

I think that is the ultimate goal of Thoreau, to live on air. That's why I said he's aesthetic, clearing out all of the dross, all of the gross material things that prevent us from being pure spirit, from living on air.

This accounts for a lot of facets of his life. I think it's not unrelated to his solitude. I don't think he's cut out for close proximity with other people. There's a very fascinating account of his meeting with Walt Whitman. He was shocked by Whitman's sexual frankness. He couldn't believe it, that this man could write about sexual intercourse, about the body. There's what the French call *pudere* in Thoreau. Don't talk about certain kinds of body processes. It's not nice. That certainly is a limit in some ways on his work.

This body of work, as I said, is clothed in a style that is quite astonishing. This man is a great creator of one-liners, some of which are famous. "The mass of men lead lives of quiet desperation." I've suggested that there's a kind of manic intensity in that remark. That we are all smoldering, that we've all settled, willy-nilly, consciously or not, for lives of repression, that the roles that we play, the domestic ones, the professional ones, these roles are killing us. I think that line conveys all of that. Other lines—one of my favorites—one of his great lines, "I have traveled a good deal in Concord." What does that mean? He's not saying I've traveled a good deal in Texas or I've traveled a good deal in New York. "I've traveled a good deal in Concord." Now, if we know anything about Concord—not a very big place. So, what is he doing in this remark? I think when you finish *Walden* you understand what he's saying. Concord is enormous. Walden Pond is going to end up being the universe; so that, after you stop chuckling about that line, "I have traveled a good deal in Concord," you begin to sense its truth that he's getting at something. You don't have to buy airplane tickets. You don't have to take steamship travels. You don't have to trek across the continent to travel. There're other kinds of travel, just as there are other kinds of ownership than having things or materially doing them.

Like the famed line, "If a man does not keep pace with his companions, perhaps it's because he hears a different drummer." This is all the language of a person who really had as a flair for what I call one-liners, for the pithy remarks that stay in our mind. He's a muscular writer. He's a visceral writer. I want to give you one or two brief instances of that, of a style that is, I think, quite wonderful. This is interesting, this one, because it's so related to one of our current infatuations, about getting people to stop smoking.

> My excuse for not lecturing against the use of tobacco is, that I never chewed it, that's a penalty which reformed tobacco-chewers have to pay; (They have to go and lecture against it) though there are things enough I have chewed which I could lecture against. If you should ever be betrayed into any of these philanthropies, (like some cause that you're going to go and lecture for) do not let your left hand know what your right hand does, for it is not worth knowing. (Now it starts to get funny) Rescue the drowning and tie your shoestrings.

No other person on earth could've written that line. "Rescue the drowning and tie your shoestrings." Rescue the drowning is the philanthropic noble cause for mankind. Don't forget about your shoestrings. You may trip over yourself before you get to the water even. Take your time and set about some free labor. There's a kind of vernacular ease in this language, about not forgetting what's really close to home, not getting distracted by the grand causes. I feel like a lot of Thoreau gets measured this way.

I called him a humorist, and I think that it's not dark humor, but there's a kind of wonderful sense of sly humor. For example,

> When I ask for a garment of a particular form, my tailoress tells me gravely, "They do not make them so now," not emphasizing the "They" at all, as if she quoted an authority

as impersonal as the Fates, and I find it difficult to get made what I want, simply because she cannot believe that I mean what I say, that I am so rash. When I hear this oracular sentence, (You remember the sentence, "they do not make them so now.") I am for a moment absorbed in thought, emphasizing to myself each word separately that I may come at the meaning of it, that I may find out by what degree of consanguinity They are related to me, and by what authority they may have in an affair which affects me so nearly; and, finally, I am inclined to answer her with an equal mystery, and without any more emphasis on the "they"—"It is true, they did not make them so recently, but they do now."

This is the tongue in cheek Thoreau who has fun with folks. He picks up that industriousness of his moment and turns it to his own purposes as well. I've already talked about the very serious economic principle in *Walden*, about the cost of things is the amount of life you have to give up to get them, but it can be more humorous than that. It can be humorous in a sentence like this.

For many years, I was self-appointed inspector of snow-storms and rain-storms, (like somebody really hired him to do this) and did my duty faithfully; surveyor, if not of highways, then of forest paths and all across-lot routes, keeping them open.

Or,

Finding that my fellow-citizens were not likely to offer me any room in the court house, or any curacy or living anywhere else, but I must shift for myself, I turned my face more exclusively than ever to the woods, where I was better known. (Great line. I've got my contacts in the woods. That's where my people are going to help me out.) I determined to go into business at once, and not wait to acquire the usual capital, using such slender means as I had already got. My purpose in going to Walden Pond was not to live cheaply nor to live dearly there, but to transact some private business with the fewest obstacles.

Watch the way that business metaphor then is really getting worked out in a very serious and yet very funny way. We'd like to think that going to the woods for a year is not quite the same as getting a job done. It doesn't sound like it's responsible labor in the same way that certainly mid-19th century would have looked at it. He's telling you, "Yes it is."

Some of the funniest passages here are in how Thoreau deals with other people. He's not, as I said, much of a philanthropic type. He doesn't particularly like folks. He talks about people in the chapter called "Visitors."

> Finally, there were the self-styled reformers, the greatest bores of all, who thought that I was forever singing,—
>
> This is the house that I built;
>
> This is the man that lives in the house that I built; but they did not know that the third line was,
>
> These are the folks that worry the man
>
> That lives in the house that I built.

He comes back. He circles around behind you and nails people. Or, in another one that it seems to me to have a certain amount of humor in it, "A lady once offered me a mat." It sounds like a fairly innocuous thing to do. He's living in pretty sparse circumstances, lives just in a very, very sparse and spare cabin in Walden. "A lady once offered me a mat, but as I had no room to spare within the house nor time to spare within or without to shake it, I declined it, preferring to wipe my feet on the sod before my door. It is best to avoid the beginnings of evil." He's not going to take even the first half step, not even a little toe step, towards sociability and others.

There's also a kind of economy in his language here that I think has some very funny effects as well. "The amount of it is, if a man is alive, there is always danger that he may die, though the danger must be allowed to be less in proportion as he is dead and alive to begin with. A man sits as many risks as he runs." We all know that metaphor about running risk. "A man sits as many risks as he runs." Or, Thoreau the great iconoclast has this to say about common sense. "Why level downward to our dullest perception always and praise that as common sense? The commonest sense is the sense of men asleep, which they express by snoring." That's what common sense is. There's a kind of laconic, sardonic one-upmanship that plays throughout this text.

I think there's also a lot of poetry in this text, and that's really what I'd like to get into now. There's a sense in which this text is wonderfully metaphoric and wonderfully obedient to Emerson's principles about words being conduits of spirit. This is how he talks about the earth.

> The soil, it appears, is suited to the seed, for it has sent its radicle downward, it may now send its shoot upward also with confidence. Why has man rooted himself thus firmly in the earth, but that he may rise in the same proportion into the heavens above?—for the nobler plants are valued for the fruit they bear at last in the air and light, far from the ground...

You remember in the last lecture, I said he goes down to bedrock, he goes up to the heavens. This is what it means to take a metaphor of the seed that sends its plant up from the earth into the air and to see that as a figure for human life. Yes, we are grounded, embedded in the earth, but only so that we may rise into the heavens. Both of those spheres belong to us. As I said, he reaches certain effects occasionally with this kind of language. He can speak of the grass in similar ways, that when the grass comes up in the spring—the "Spring" chapter is one of his most magnificent chapters in *Walden*—and the color green as being the color of the sun as he's concerned. He speaks of the whole life process of how the grass is then mown and then set aside to become hay for the animals, how it continues in each of its permutations, each of its phases, to be the living source of life. "So our human life but dies down to its root— our human life, but dies down to its root, and still puts forth its green blade to eternity." All of a sudden this description of natural process, grass, hay, animals, becomes richly metaphoric for the human enterprise that ultimately is aimed at eternity.

Walden is about claiming our estate, much as Emerson's work is, and it's about enjoying paradise, but seeing that paradise is right here. In one of his most famous and beautiful lines, he writes this: "Time is but the stream a go a-fishing in. I drink at it." Notice how totally metaphoric this is. I fish in time, I drink in it. "But while I drink, I see the sandy bottom and detect how shallow it is. Its thin current slides away, but eternity remains. I would drink deeper, fish in the sky," what a line, "drink deeper, fish in the sky, whose bottom is pebbly with stars." He's going to fish in the sky.

Now he has totally inverted the realms of the stream and the heavens. He'll fish in the sky, and he sees that the bottom of the sky is pebbly with stars. What a way of appropriating the universe, of domesticating it, of bringing it into his own organic tropes here. "…fish in the sky, whose bottom is pebbly with stars. I cannot count one. I know not the first letter of the alphabet." The stars of the sky that I see in the water that I want to fish in to get my nurturance in, I've learned nothing ever about that. I can't count those things. I can't name those things. "I have always been regretting that I was not as wise as the day I was born." I was born knowing those things. I was born initiated into that. All of the so-called learning, wisdom, smarts, shrewdness, practicality, that my society has taught me has made me illiterate.

Here is the elemental language. I mean my words here, the language of the elements, that we are to master and to learn. It's right here, not even at our doorstep. It's under us and it's over us. The wonderful mobility of that passage, "to fish in the sky whose bottom is pebbly with stars" is why I call him a poet. There is much extravagant language in *Walden*. There's much mock epic in *Walden*, where the experience at Walden Pond becomes Homeric. This is how he describes mosquitoes:

> Morning brings back the heroic ages. I was as much affected by the faint hum of a mosquito making its invisible and (that's because he's trying to imagine) unimaginable tour through my apartment at earliest dawn, when I was sitting with door and windows open, as I could be by any trumpet that ever sang of fame. It was Homer's requiem; itself an *Iliad* and *Odyssey* in the air, singing its own wrath and wanderings. (That's the rephrasing of the first words of the *Iliad*.) There was something cosmical about it; a standing advertisement, till forbidden, of the everlasting vigor and fertility of the world.

No other human being has ever said this about the buzzing noise of a mosquito. Most of us hide for cover or look for the villain. But in his case, it becomes transformed into Homeric epithet, into this splendid display of life, unimaginable tour of this insect. This way of transforming the minute activities of the birds and the bees is further developed in a very famous sequence, which is about the war of the ants. As you can imagine, he observes red ants and black ants at war,

and again, automatically, he thinks of Homer. He thinks of the *Iliad*.
He thinks of the Greeks and the Trojans. So he describes this fight,
and he describes it with a remarkable detail.

> On every side they were engaged in deadly combat, yet
> without any noise that I could hear, and human soldiers
> never fought so resolutely. I watched a couple that were fast
> locked in each other's embraces, in a little sunny valley amid
> the chips, now at noonday prepared to fight till the sun went
> down, or life went out. The smaller red champion had
> fastened himself like a vice to his adversary's front, and
> through all the tumblings on that field never for an instant
> ceased to gnaw at one of his feelers near the root, having
> already caused the other to go by the board; while the
> stronger black one dashed him from side to side, and, as I
> saw on looking nearer, had already divested him of several
> of his members. They fought with more pertinacity than
> bulldogs. Neither manifested the least disposition to retreat.
> It was evident that their battle-cry was "Conquer or die."

He reflects on all of this. The more you think of it, the less the
difference. Certainly, there is not the fight recorded in conquered
history, and conquered after all is the site of a very important battle.

> …there is not the fight recorded in Concord history, at least,
> if in the history of America, that will bear a moment's
> comparison with this, whether for the numbers engaged in it,
> (Look at how many people are dying in this battle) or for the
> patriotism and heroism displayed. For numbers and for
> carnage it was an Austerlitz or Dresden. Concord Fight!

He describes, you know, with grisly anatomical detail, this combat. It
points to something grand. I called it mock epic, but mock epic is
what you have in Pope and other writers where there's a satirical
intent. I don't think this is satirical at all. These are ways in which
the stay at Walden Pond for one year becomes an arena for
magnificent events. Every day, every moment—if you have the eyes
and wit to take it in—you are seeing grandeur, you are seeing
splendor, and you are seeing courage. That's what the natural species
exhibits all the time. There's a feeling in this text and you can see
these are language things. After all, the ants do not tell him to reflect
on Homer. He looks at this, and he brings all of his own learning, his

being grounded in the classics, as a way to show you something of the actual scale and excitement of these natural events.

If you can see that about mosquitoes and about ants, then you're really not living quite as solitary, hermitlike life as has been thought. It is true that he is something of a misanthrope that he has not much love lost for the human neighbors or visitors that he receives, or for the people in the village. But it's also true that he makes the woods into something rich and strange. It's as if the woods become a new kind of cosmos for him, and that he sees the life that goes on. In some wonderful passages, he traces the chain of being. He looks at an abandoned farm. He has wonderful remarks about how sad it is to see an abandoned well. He evokes the life of the people who live there, who are long dead now, and this place is a ruin. He closes by saying, This is the abandoned farm.

> Still grows the vivacious lilac a generation after the door and lintel and the sill are gone, unfolding its sweet-scented flowers each spring, to be plucked by the musing traveler; planted and tended once by the children's hands, in front-yard plots—now standing by wallsides in retired pastures, and giving place to new-rising forests…

And the lilac that was planted, slender tiny plants that the children were probably sent out by the parents to do, the children themselves are now dead, the farm is abandoned, and you have these wonderful lilac trees that are growing there. He talks about that. He talks about that as a language.

> Little did the dusky children think that the puny slip with its two eyes only, which they stuck in the ground in the shadow of the house and daily watered, would root itself so, and outlive them, and the house itself in the rear that shaded it, and grown man's garden and orchard, and tell their story faintly to the lone wanderer (that's him) a half-century after they had grown up and died—blossoming as fair, smelling as sweet, as in that first spring. I mark its still tender, civil, cheerful lilac colors.

That's what I call "the chain of being." To tell a story, is the way he puts it, tell their story. It's as if the growths in nature, the living and dying and rebirth and natural process, tells us over and over about human duration. He can afford to be cold and callous about the people who come to visit him. He still is always talking about life. He uses this wonderful phrase, "repeopled," with such reminiscences, "I repeopled the woods and lulled myself asleep." He says things like, "Frequently I tramped eight or 10 miles through the deepest snow to keep an appointment with a beech tree or a yellow birch, or an old acquaintance among the pines." There is a social dimension to this text. It's displaced, we might say. We don't know exactly what its community benefit is likely to be. It nonetheless exists. In one of his most wonderful passages, he admires the birds that sing, and he says, "Who knows but that if men constructed their dwellings with their own hands and provided food for themselves and their families simply and honestly enough, the poetic faculty would be universally developed as birds universally sing when they are so engaged?" And I'll close with that reference. Birds that sing as they construct their nests, working, singing, this is put forth as a model for human life. They're not separable.

Lecture Nine
Walden—Yesterday, Today, and Tomorrow

Scope:

Thoreau enters the American canon belatedly, and his celebration of nature was thought to be sentimental and dated, whereas his politics have been seminal, reappearing in Gandhi and Martin Luther King. Now, in an age of environmental awareness and nature writing, Thoreau's views on Walden Pond may well constitute a politics of their own. Thoreau's importance as writer transcends the ideological, however, because he has fashioned a breathtaking new language for portraying the life cycle itself in its natural processes. The most staggering passages in *Walden* seem to map out a new language and a new vision: to tell the human story and take the human measure by dint of a purely natural language. Thoreau's paean to spring, to the surging life force and life forms that he sees at Walden Pond, constitutes a radically new kind of discourse; this is his vision of hope.

Objectives: Upon completion of this lecture, you should be able to:

1. Explain Thoreau's notion of the relationship between nature and culture.

2. Summarize Thoreau's use of reading as a metaphor in Walden.

3. Explain Thoreau's vision of nature as a living hieroglyph.

Outline

I. Thoreau's reputation within the American canon has changed radically over the years.

   A. In the 19th century, he was seen largely as an eccentric, a marginal figure in Emerson's shadow.

   B. In the 1920s, Modernism redefined the American canon and foreshadowed the notion of political and cultural dissent.

   1. Enter Thoreau the political writer, while Longfellow and Lowell, much admired by their peers, are shoved out.

   2. American literature comes to be seen in terms of visionary dissent, and at last there is recognition for neglected figures. Thoreau benefits from this move.

II. Thoreau the environmental prophet is a singularly topical figure in today's cultural climate.

    A. "Small is better" is not a Thoreau quotation, but he might indeed have said it. One feels peevishness in his work, a mania just under the surface, a willingness to promote this and to proscribe that. These are recognizable features of modern "political correctness."

        1. Forgo animal flesh; live on air. Thoreau supported these maxims, and we can easily imagine t-shirts printed with these mottoes.

        2. Thoreau's distrust of material clutter, his sense that our possessions, no less than the animal flesh we consume, clog our arteries, would make him an appropriate contemporary spokesman.

        3. Thoreau's richest insight is that real ownership—far from having anything to do with money or possessions—is imaginative.

    B. Nature, according to Thoreau, is our true home.

        1. We are *of* nature, Thoreau argues, and most of our "civilized" concepts reflect a tragic distance and alienation from the natural scene.

        2. Much of the point of *Walden* is that we have never *seen* nature, in the shimmering immediacy with which it is delivered in this writing.

    C. The beauty of Walden Pond emerges as the unstated message of the work.

        1. Thoreau is at pains to show us that, of all the Massachusetts ponds, Walden is the fairest of them all.

        2. In musing about the inhabitants and history of this pond, Thoreau suggests that nature is also a chronicle of the history of the planet; nature is written on by culture.

    D. The fate of Walden Pond is an issue that is far more melancholy to today's readers than it was to Thoreau himself, who sensed the threats of civilization but could hardly imagine their virulence.

    E. In depicting the remarkable life of the pond, Thoreau shows us that nature does not die, but the ruins of civilization are nonetheless green.

F. Perhaps the great lesson of *Walden* is that we must learn to *read*. Thoreau suggests that nature wants to "tell" her story that she is rich in signs for us to interpret.

III. The story of Walden is Thoreau's great triumph: this pond is not simply a pond, but a story, a work of art.

A. Walden lives through Thoreau, as every reader of his text has both discovered and made happen.

B. Thoreau comes to us, then, not as historian, but as *creator* of Walden, and this act of creation is replete with sights and sounds.

1. In some fascinating passages, Thoreau recreates the actual sounds of life on the pond.

2. Other passages convey the strange life and vitality of this place, such as the whooping of the ice and the gambit of the foxes.

3. Thoreau the surveyor spends much time taking Walden's measure, and although we may initially find such work mundane, we soon see the mythical stakes: he is measuring the secret of the universe, the riddle of the sphinx.

4. Walden—finally measured, mapped, and represented— is more than a pond; it turns out to be a personal code for delivering our own story, for mapping the human figure.

5. The most amazing sequence in *Walden* focuses on the form and function of nature's simplest item, the leaf. In devising a language for this evolving and repeating natural form, Thoreau fashions a strange new biological code and reveals nature to be a living hieroglyph.

6. In *Walden* we see the genesis of a man, but unlike in Mary Shelley's *Frankenstein*, man evolves from organic matter.

C. Thoreau leaves us with the account of his year, but it ends in openness, not closure: *Walden* is a springtime, sap-flowing, wake-up call to its readers.

1. Thoreau closes his text with a famous account of daybreak, enabling us to see him properly as a prophet of Dawn.

2. In thinking through the contrast between art and environment, between Walden Pond and Thoreau's

Walden, we realize that the future can indeed be built with a book, for language survives the encroachments of civilization.

Readings:

Essential: Thoreau, *Walden* (Library of America, 1985)

Recommended: Matthiessen, *American Renaissance* (Oxford University Press, 1941); Kazin, *An American Procession* (Vintage, 1985)

Topics for Further Consideration:

1. Explain how you would answer the charge that Thoreau is nothing but derivative Emerson.

2. Thoreau's project of confronting life at Walden Pond has the makings of an American myth. Explain whether you see evidence of this myth in subsequent American literature and in American life today.

Lecture Nine—Transcript
Walden—Yesterday, Today, and Tomorrow

This is Lecture Nine, and it's the last of my three lectures on Thoreau, and therefore would be appropriate to try to do pretty much what he does. That is to say, he takes the measure of Walden Pond and of Walden woods, in his book and I will try, in some ways, to take his measure and to leave you with a sense of that, in this lecture—but not in any kind of programmatic surveying way. I'd rather take the measure of *Walden* on terms that seem to me to be most interesting, which is the art of this text. This is what I mean: one of the most fascinating things about Thoreau is that he appears as one of our first writers on the environment, with all of the drama that's packed into that, the fragility of natural systems, the encroachment of an industrial society that is not really much in view when he's writing, but that we have known, or learned so much of in the 150 years since.

I want to bring to bear the issue of what lives and what dies, how natural systems can be threatened, how efforts are made by environmentalists to protect and to steward nature; but also, to bring into the equation how art plays a role in this—this art. After all, *Walden* is both a place and a text. They each have their own kind of life and death. I want to get into that. I'd like to backtrack and to try to position Thoreau in the canon once again—the canon of American writers—because it sheds some light on the importance of the environmental theme in his work. In the 19th century, as I've repeated, he was thought of as an eccentric; as a quack. His books hardly sold. *A Week on the Concord and Merrimack Rivers* sold so badly, was such a non-seller— and he was still revising it, when it finally came out—that he took back 706 of the 1,000 copies. He wrote to a friend, "I now have a library of nearly 900 volumes, over 700 of which, I wrote myself."

At the time of his work, his views on the environment, on nature, what they called his "Naturism," was considered conventional, because these issues did not have the kind of cosmic threat that they have to us today. His philosophy, as I've said, was considered derivative Emerson. He begins to become important in the 1920s. Thoreau comes in as Emerson moves out, because of his dissent position in American culture. He looks like a kind of visionary. Still, people didn't know what to do with the nature material. What is interesting here—and the reason that I've put these pieces in place—is that for us, Thoreau the defender of nature, the chanter of nature, and Thoreau the political dissenter, in *Civil Disobedience*, are the same person, because nature is a political cause for us. That's what environmentalism is about. That's one of the strongest arenas where people have to show great courage and have to take on formidable adversaries.

In a sense, Thoreau makes more and more sense, the pieces fit together more and more today, than they could have a century ago, or even 50 years ago. *Walden* has been rightly thought of as one of the great pastoral texts in literature. Usually, in the Renaissance, pastoral was an affair of shepherds and shepherdesses. People who lived in the woods never wrote it. Pastoral is a city product. People who lived in London, imagined trysts in the woods, disguised as shepherds and shepherdesses. It's a way to invent the woods in order to then recreate a vantage point on your own society, and on your own culture. I think Thoreau is pastoral in that sense. He doesn't have the conventions of pastoral, but he uses the woods and *Walden* as a way of achieving another view on the world of the mid-19th century.

Some of this, I've already alluded to. Some of his slogans—some of his pet causes—are our causes. One of his phrases, "Shall we always study to obtain more of these things, and not sometimes to be content with less?" We've heard that in the last 20 or 30 years, that small is better; less is better than more. This is not unrelated to ecological thinking and the amount of natural resources that an environment has? Other features of Thoreau, "Forego animal flesh," "Live on air." These are things that we could find on t-shirts today. Thoreau constantly promotes a view of ownership as imaginative, rather than material. He wants to liberate people from the kind of material chains that they're under, and he can be very funny about it. You remember a passage in an earlier lecture, where he lambasted this farmer, who's given his name to this pond, and here is a comparable passage:

> I have frequently seen a poet withdraw, having enjoyed the most valuable part of a farm, while the crusty farmer supposed that he had got a few wild apples only. Why, the owner does not know it for many years when a poet has put his farm in rhyme, the most admirable kind of invisible

fence, has fairly impounded it, milked it, skimmed it, and got all the cream, and left the farmer only the skimmed milk.

That by translating it, transforming the material world into something spiritual—and we're close to again Emersonian linguistics here—by taking natural facts and having us understand them as spiritual facts, or transforming them into language, that too is a form of ownership. It's a form of possession. He very much resembles Emerson in this regard.

Thoreau tells us over and over, that the natural world is our home, and sometimes he puts this in quite beautiful phrases: "Why should I feel lonely? Is not our planet in the Milky Way?" This is my family. I look at the Milky Way, and I see home. "I see the place that I'm part of." He tells us over and over that we are of nature. "Shall I not have intelligence with the earth? Am I not partly leaves and vegetable mold, myself?" And yet, he knows quite well, that for most of us, we've never seen this. We haven't discovered our fit in nature. We haven't really looked.

It's surprising and memorable, as well as a valuable experience to be lost in the woods anytime.

> Often in a snow-storm, even by day, one will come out upon a well-known road and yet find it impossible to tell which way leads to the village. Though he knows that he has traveled it a thousand times, he cannot recognize a feature in it, but it is as strange to him as if it were a road in Siberia. By night, of course, the perplexity is infinitely greater. In our most trivial walks, we are constantly, though unconsciously, steering like pilots by certain well-known beacons and headlands, and if we go beyond our usual course we still carry in our minds the bearing of some neighboring cape…

By the way, this has been borne out by anthropologists, people who have checked on even nomadic tribes the way in which we carry in our minds, homing devices, and we unconsciously have markers so that's how you find your way home, all the time. You only need to see two or three sights that will tell you, confirm for you, that you're on your way. For the most part, if any of us was asked to describe in detail what our 15-minute walk home looks like, we couldn't, because what we really only have is two or three things that are the beacons for us. I think Thoreau is trying to get at that. Not until we are completely lost, or turned around, "For a man needs only to be turned around once with his eyes shut in the world, to be lost," do we appreciate the vastness, and strangeness of nature. Not until we're lost—in other words, not 'til we have lost the world—do we begin to find ourselves and realize where we are in the infinite extent of our relations.

So, we've never seen things. We're too blinded by routine, habit, perceptual schemes that shut out, rather than bring in, reality to us. Walden Pond is over and over, described in this book, in fresh, vivid, intrusive ways. It jumps at us. We realize this man is seeing this body of water in such a way as to make us see it, so that we don't simply walk past it, as it were, texturally. "It is the fairest pond of all. In such a day in September or October, Walden is a perfect forest mirror." Notice it's already going to work metaphorically. It's going to reflect other things. It's a forest mirror. It's not just the pond itself, it's what it brings into our purview. "Set round with stones as precious to my eye, as if fewer or rarer. Nothing so fair, so pure, and at the same time so large as a lake, per chance, lies on the surface of the earth. Sky, water…" And here we have, once again, this wonderful inversion of terms. It brings us the sky. We see the sky now, as liquid. We could fish in it. The stars are the pebbles. It needs no fence. Nations can come and go, without defiling it. There, of course, as modern readers, we read that with a certain tug, since we know that nations come and go, and we do defile our lakes, and our ponds.

The fate of Walden Pond, as we all know, hasn't always been a happy fate. There are famous photographs of Walden Pond, surrounded by places where they sell sandwiches, cokes, littered with beer cans. That Walden Pond, despite the pristine purity that it has in Thoreau's 19th century evocation, has suffered the same ravages— hot-dog stands, pollution, photographers—as any other site. In some scary, irony, Thoreau is responsible. Walden Pond has become a site of tourism because of Thoreau's own beautiful text. Art can kill, as well as celebrate. That doesn't mean that nature itself can die, as the passage that I read about the lilacs that continue to grow even after the farm has died, and the people and the children have grown up and died. This green language of nature knows no death, and that's the story that Thoreau wants to tell. He says that these lilacs are telling a story, if we know how to read it.

That leads to me what to me, is most interesting, ultimately, and enduring about this text, which is the life of Walden. Walden text. Life comes through the language of this text. It's not really accurate to say that Thoreau describes Walden. What I want to tell you is, that Thoreau creates Walden. This is what artists always do. He makes it for us. He makes it live for us, as it lived for him. He does this in countless different ways, and I'm going to try to describe some of them for you. One of the liveliest, most charming passages, he conveys to us the sounds of the pond. This could be, of course, one of the great roles of literature, to convert nature into language—to hear the natural world, and then to convey it. He talks about being around the pond in the evening, around the woods.

> Hoo hoo hoo, hoorer, hoo, sounded sonorously, and the first three syllables accented somewhat like how der do; or sometimes hoo hoo only. One night in the beginning of winter, before the pond froze over, about nine o'clock, I was startled by the loud honking of a goose, and, stepping to the door, I heard the sound of their wings like a tempest in the woods as they flew low over my house. They passed over the pond toward Fair Haven, seemingly deterred from settling by my light, their commodore honking, all the while with a regular beat. Suddenly an unmistakable cat-owl from very near me, with the most harsh and tremendous voice I ever heard from any inhabitant of the woods, responded at regular intervals to the goose, as if determined to expose and disgrace this intruder from Hudson's Bay by exhibiting a greater compass and volume of voice in a native, and boo-hoo him out of Concord horizon. What do you mean by alarming the citadel at this time of night consecrated to me? Do you think I am ever caught napping at such an hour, that I have not got lungs and a larynx as well as you? Boo-hoo, boo-hoo, boo-hoo!

It's one of the most thrilling discords I ever heard. Yet, if you had a discriminating ear, there were in it, the elements of a Concord. He's playing with where he is, Concord, Massachusetts, these noises, discord, a concord that he's hearing.

> …the elements of a concord such as these plains never saw nor heard. I also heard the whooping of the ice in the pond, my great bed-fellow in that part of Concord, as if it were

restless in its bed and would fain turn over... Sometimes, I heard the foxes as they ranged over the snow-crust, in moonlight nights, in search of a partridge or other game, barking raggedly and demonically like forest dogs, as if laboring with some anxiety, or seeking expression, struggling for light and to be dogs outright and run freely in the streets; for if we take the ages into our account, may there not be a civilization going on among brutes as well as men? They seemed to me to be rudimental, burrowing men, still standing on their defense, awaiting their transformation.

Ovid could've written these lines. It sounds like *The Metamorphoses*. This is an oral account of Concord woods, of Walden woods, of Walden Pond, and in it is all of these messages, all of the commerce, all of the intercourse of the various inhabitants of the woods. Some from far away, from Hudson's Bay, some defenders of the turf, the geese, and then the foxes, and then the ice joins in. "Bedfellow" he calls it. This is what it means when he says, "I have repeopled the woods." Those sounds, and I tried to read it in such a way as to emphasize those sounds, are the life of this text. That's the life of these woods. The woods as voice, Walden as a voice that we are meant to understand.

Walden, for him, becomes the riddle of the Sphinx. It becomes—you recall that image presented by Emerson, that every great writer has confronted nature just as Oedipus confronted the Sphinx, and been asked to explain the riddle? Each great text that we read is an effort to decode or translate natural splendor—natural mystery—into language. Well, that's essentially the function of Walden Pond. It works that way. For example, this text actually has maps of Thoreau's measuring of the pond. He takes its measures. As I said in this lecture, I want to try to do what he does, take the measure of things. In taking the measure of the pond, Thoreau once again—in good Emersonian fashion—moves from the material to the spiritual or metaphorical. He has talked, for example, about measuring the diameter of the pond in two different places, so as to get its full circumference.

> Such a rule of the two diameters not only guides us towards the sun in the system (the solar system) and the heart in man, but draws lines through the length and breadth of the aggregate of a man's particular daily behaviors and waves of

life into his coves and inlets, and where they intersect will be the height or depth of his character.

Remarkable line! That we could, in fact, map ourselves this way. That we could take our particular diameters, the coves that we go into, and measure the depth of them. Here is the metaphor of Walden, the metaphor of the pond, being used as a way of graphing human life. That's what's going to happen over and over in the finest chapters here. We will see that the lines that separate the human from the natural, from the spiritual, are systematically blurred, eroded or transgressed, so that we go from one into the other. That's the heroic view of language that Emerson prescribed, that nature is a sign of spirit, words are signs of nature, and words themselves are to lead us to spirit. Thoreau, I think, keeps his end of the bargain.

I want to spend a couple of minutes with one of the most astounding and difficult sequences in all of *Walden*, and it's significantly in the chapter called "Spring." Thoreau celebrates the thawing out of Walden Pond, of Walden woods, and he shows us, in ways that I've never seen before, what these processes look like. I want you to bear in mind what I said a minute ago, that the lines, the conceptual lines that we think separate the natural from the human from the lingual— from language—all of these things are going to be fused together in this sequence. He's talking about the sap that starts to flow, the water that seems to come out of the earth, and the new forms. There's really a remarkable sense of morphology in what I'm going to read to you.

"No wonder," he says, "that the earth expresses itself outwardly in leaves." That's going to be the central issue here. "The earth expresses itself outwardly in leaves." You recall that "leaves" is a term that has been used for books and things like that, and that's a concept, or a conceit that's going to be very, very serious here. Of course, there is papyrus. Books themselves seem to have come as part of the end stage of nature. "It so labors with the idea inwardly, the atoms have already learned this law, and are pregnant by the overhanging leaf sees here, its prototype. Internally, whether in the globe, or animal body, it is a moist, thick *lobe*." Now, listen to what's happening here. He's going to start taking words. *Lobe* is in italics. He's going to tell you how they sound, and how they are spelled.

"It is a moist, thick *lobe*. A word especially applicable to the liver, and lungs, and leaves of fat." And he gives the Greek term, which I can't pronounce. Then, he gives Latin terms, *labor, lapsus*, to flow or slip downward, a lapsing, and another Greek term. "*Globus*, then lobe, globe, also lap, flap, and many other words, externally a dry, thin leaf." Think about the word leaf. Visualize it. L-e-a-f. "Even as the f and v, are a pressed and dry b, the radicals of lobe are *lob-* And the soft mass of the *b*, single *lobed*, or *B*, the full capital *B*, double-lobed, with a liquid *L* behind it, pressing it forward." This is really taking natural phenomena and forcing it into script. Or showing us that it is script. This is hieroglyphics in front of our eyes.

"In globe, *glob*, the guttural *g* adds to the meaning, the capacity of the throat. The feathers and the wings of birds are drier and thinner leaves." What a remarkable statement! The feathers and wings of birds are drier and thinner leaves. This is a kind of process of transformation. It's really like the processes that we think of with butterflies. He's going to say that. "You pass from the lumpish grub in the earth, to the airy and fluttering butterfly."

He goes on to describe, in kind of extraordinary detail, what he sees happening in spring. He talks about the salacious matter, which water deposits. He calls it the bony system. He talks about fleshly fiber and cellular tissue that is related to soil and organic matter. "What is man but a mass of thawing clay?" Now, he's going to talk about the human body. "The bowl of the human finger, is but a drop congealed." What does that mean? "The fingers and the toes flow to their extent, from the thawing mass of the body." We think of our body as fixed, finite, stable, and static. No! It's part of spring. It's part of this process. It seems only now to have stopped at our extremities. It doesn't have to be that way. The fingers and the toes flow to their extent.

"Who knows what the human body would expand and flow out to, under a more genial heaven. Is not the hand, a spreading palm leaf, with its lobes and veins?" Think about your hand as a leaf with lobes and veins. These are the same words that he's been talking about. "The ear," think about what an ear is.

> The ear may be regarded, fancifully, as a lichen, *umbilicaria*, on the side of the head, with its lobe or drop. The lip— *labium*, from labor (?)—(the same terms coming over and over here) laps or lapses from the sides of the cavernous

mouth. The nose is a manifest congealed drop or stalactite. The chin is a still larger drop, the confluent dripping of the face. The cheeks are a slide from the brows into the valley of the face, opposed and diffused by the cheek bones. Each rounded lobe of the vegetable leaf, too, is a thick and now loitering drop, larger or smaller; the lobes are the fingers of the leaf...

It's an astonishing metamorphic passage, in which the human figure, the human body, the human parts, are all seen as one organic flux that is replicated in nature, as the thaw comes, and the vital juices of the earth become visible, and things reshape and reform. Even more miraculously, replicated in words, in etymology, in terms, in the way we use language. This is organic language. This is hieroglyphics, if it ever existed. What I just read you is about the making of a man. Quite unlike *Frankenstein*—the famous text where dead body parts are put together in a kind of fantasy of science—here we have organic material that is in nature, in Walden Pond, and we see genesis. Not the way the Bible has it, but we see it nonetheless, coming out of the materials of the earth, of the woods, and finally culminating in the human body.

It's a remarkable tribute. It's about the making of a human being. Isn't that what *Walden* is? That's what the whole project has been. It's about the making of a human being. How to become a real human being. That's what this trip to the woods was all about. This text then, is a text about becoming human, being reborn. As he frequently says, "Waking up at last," because we have been "long asleep." A metaphor that has been with us ever since *Rip Van Winkle*. It's not easy to wake up, but we must believe that we can.

"That man who does not believe that each day contains an earlier, more sacred and auroral hour, than he has yet profaned, has despaired of life, and is pursuing a descending and darkening way." Or, "To be awake is to be alive! I have never yet met a man who is quite awake. How could I have looked him in the face?" What a staggering notion, that someone who is fully alive, it's like looking at the sun. It's unbearable. It's raw, pure energy and life. There's a really fierce pagan passion in this work about natural process, about tapping into these rhythms, about making us see not only that they can be brought to language; but also that they are language. That's this Romantic view of language that comes across in this text.

"Wake up," is the great metaphor of the text. I'm not even sure that it's metaphoric. It's what this text urges upon us. "We are acquainted with the mere pellicle of the globe on which we live, most have not delved six feet beneath the surface, nor leaped as many above it. We know not where we are." Besides, we're nearly sound asleep, nearly half of the time. This text closes with a very famous reference about the dawn: "The light which puts out our eyes is darkness to us. Only that day dawns to which we are awake. We are dawn." Our awakening intelligence, our awakening intercourse with nature; that is dawn. There is more day to dawn. "The sun is but a morning star." That's the last line of *Walden*, but it's not where I want to close.

I'd like to close with two other references that I think allow us to move back from the heavens and the stars to Thoreau himself, on earth. He picks up an image that is a rather cheap trope about castles in the air. You've all heard it. It's used to usually describe fantasies that have no grounding in reality. "If you had built castles in the air," he says, "your work need not be lost. That's where they should be. Now put the foundation under them." It's time to put foundations under your castles in the air. How do you put a foundation under a castle in the air? Well, you use your human resources.

> The intellect is a cleaver; it discerns and rifts its way into the secret of things. I do not wish to be any more busy with my hands than is necessary. My head is hands and feet. (My head is going to do labor) I feel all my best faculties concentrated in it. My instinct tells me that my head is an organ for burrowing, as some creatures use their snout and fore paws, and with it I would mine and burrow my way through these hills. I think that the richest vein is somewhere hereabouts; so by the divining-rod and thin rising vapors I judge; and here I will begin to mine.

It's again going down in order to reach heaven.

Lecture Ten
Edgar Allan Poe

Scope:

Poe is arguably the strangest figure in the American literary landscape, and for many people the myth of Poe himself—orphan, disowned, wedded to his child-bride cousin, alcoholic, found dying in a Baltimore street—resembles his characters—yet it is more powerful than anything he wrote. He is conceivably our most influential 19th-century writer, for he impacts the literature of Europe, especially France, in such a decisive fashion that he finally returns to American shores via his influence. Poe is a figure to be reckoned with. Consider his wide realm of influence: polished Romantic poet of incomparable technical virtuosity, premier literary critic, theorist of art, creator of prophetic genres such as science fiction and the detective story, and author of those horror stories that we read when young and that we see again in our sensationalist film culture today. His work circles forever around prodigious secrets—having to do with murder, vampirism, and death of all stripes—and it is fair to say that these same poems and stories reside in our collective subconscious, waiting for us to unpack them at last.

Poe's own life story is essential to any understanding of his work, so we begin with the tortured biography, and we consider a number of important, often dismissive judgments made on his work. Poe's poetry is often slighted as being meretricious, and yet a number of these poems are literally haunting in their suggestiveness; even more certain is the impact of Poe's famous theory of literature, since it altered the course of European poetry. Finally, his notorious view that the subject of beauty *par excellence* consists of the death of a beautiful woman will be examined in his lyric, "Annabel Lee," so that we can ready ourselves for its reappearance throughout his *oeuvre*.

Objectives: Upon completion of this lecture, you should be able to:

1. Summarize Poe's contribution to the development of Modernist poetry.

2. Infer the reasons behind Poe's dissolute reputation.

3. Outline Poe's contributions to the detective story and science fiction.

Outline

I. Poe is the most maligned figure in the American canon. His swollen image as "cursed poet" seems like a fabricated cliché, whereas his actual poems and stories are too often dismissed as sensationalist.

   A. As readers of Poe's work, we must contend with his reputation as a sensitive, drunk, sick, kinky, necrophiliac gambler. We will see that these images reappear in much of his work.

   B. Charles Dickens might have written Poe's biography in a maudlin moment. This work reminds us of figures like Oliver Twist and other literary creations. The reality, however, is tougher.

      1. Born in 1809 to professional actors, Poe came literally from a histrionic background. His father abandoned his mother early, then died in 1811; his mother died later of consumption.

      2. Poe was taken into the Virginia home of John and Frances Allan; he was close to Frances Allan, but John did not adopt him.

      3. Poe's schooling took place in both Virginia and England; he later attended the University of Virginia, where he became known for a dissolute lifestyle.

      4. Poe took up the excessive drinking and gambling that he is known for (although we know that he did not always drink much but rather was excessively sensitive to the effects of alcohol). He also experienced his first failed love affair. At the end of his life, he returned to this love.

      5. Poe ran away, joined the Army, and did well. Like Poe's mother, Mrs. Allan also died of consumption, and Poe's only family connection now was John Allan, who sternly disapproved of Poe's behavior.

      6. Allan helped Poe attend West Point, where he initially did well. But a lack of funds prevented Poe from staying, and he got himself expelled. Poe then began to make his reputation by publishing poetry and stories.

      7. In 1836, Poe married Virginia Clemm, his 14-year-old cousin, his famous "child bride." Critics speculate that

Poe was impotent and that this relationship remained platonic.

8. Poe developed a substantial career as editor, poet, and critic and became famous with the publication of "The Raven."

9. Virginia died of consumption in 1846. We begin to see the pattern of loved women dying in Poe's life, which is at the core of his work.

10. In 1849, Poe succumbed to binges and sprees, was found unconscious on a Baltimore street, then died in a Baltimore hospital.

C. A complicated individual, Poe was characterized by a wide range of incompatible traits; his reputation among his literary peers varied a great deal, too.

1. He was unquestionably a man of culture, yet surprisingly on target in his view of literary reputations, he was possessed of old-fashioned Southern courtesy, but he was notoriously hard to get along with, finicky, and often extreme in his judgments.

2. Emerson referred to Poe in a conversation as "the jingle man," and this dismissive comment speaks volumes about Poe's lack of standing among the "Brahmins" of New England in the early 19th century.

3. James Russell Lowell, one of the most recognized contemporary poets of the period, characterized Poe as "fudge."

4. Walt Whitman is the only major American man of letters who attended a memorial service for Poe in the 1870s. Although he was Poe's virtual opposite, Whitman had a surprising grasp of Poe's genius.

5. Henry James, our first professional literary critic/historian, considered Poe to be distinctly minor.

6. T.S. Eliot, following James' cue, also regarded Poe as insignificant, a judgment that came to be ironic, given Poe's indirect influence on his own poetic production.

II. Poe's poems are astonishing in their technical polish and hypnotic cadences, and there is a kind of magic when we listen to "the jingle man."

A. "The Bells" is Poe's most extreme phonic experiment, a poem that maniacally repeats and captures the actual sound of bells.

    1. The subject of Poe's poem is eerily connected with its phonic character as Poe outlines the shifting meaning of bells.

    2. Repetition comes to be seen as the language of psychosis, and even in a piece like "The Bells," there is a link between technique and meaning.

B. "Eldorado" is one of Poe's briefest, most haunting pieces about man's eternal quest; the goal of which can be whatever we wish—heaven, truth, or beauty. At the same time, we know that Poe's poem of 1849 was specifically addressed to a major social event of his time, the California Gold Rush.

C. "The Raven" is, of course, Poe's most famous poem. The piece is an ingenious example of complex rhyme and metric schemes.

    1. The unforgettable first stanza sounds the Poe note: an intrusive messenger, a weird new music.

    2. Parrot-like, the raven has only one obsessive word, "Nevermore." Poe's piece repeats this refrain like a recurring nightmare, and it conjures up an entire philosophy of doom, of a haunting yet irretrievable past.

III. Poe's great contribution to literary theory is his conception of Poet as Maker vs. Poet as Seer; in this we see a drastic calling-into-question of Romantic assumptions.

A. "The Philosophy of Composition" or "How I Wrote the Raven" (1846) is the (perhaps spoofing) famous account of Poe's poetic practice.

    1. Every effect is planned, according to Poe. In poetry, there are no accidents, no effects of inspiration. We foolishly persist in thinking that poetry is spontaneous, whereas it is strategic.

    2. Poe goes on to define the ideal subjects of poetry: beauty, melancholy, and death. The consequences of this notion are extreme and predictable—the great subject must be, as one could easily guess, the death of a beautiful woman. We shall see that this "literary theory" is utterly consonant with Poe's own tragic biography.

3. Poe is splendidly technical in his essay; he shows us exactly how and why the refrain and metric scheme of "The Raven" are as they are.

B. The French reaction to Poe's manifesto is of great significance because he gets a hearing across the ocean that is denied to him at home. Thus, a new aesthetic is born.

1. Baudelaire, the greatest French poet of the 19th century, seizes on the work and career of Poe as the epitome of genius; Baudelaire becomes Poe's champion/translator. As the founder of symbolism in poetry, Baudelaire assures Poe's continued impact on poetic development.

2. Poe serves as the central "cargo" in a famous, documented "chain" of poetic influence, moving from Baudelaire to Mallarmé, and Valéry, on to T.S. Eliot, and back to America.

IV. Despite critics' carping, Poe is America's most influential 19th-century man of letters.

A. Modern poetry, as indicated, is demonstrably in his debt.

B. Poe essentially created the detective story; he considers the powers of ratiocination as the opposite pole to pure sensation. This "split" marks much of his thinking.

1. Auguste Dupin, Poe's genial Parisian detective, reigns in Poe's seminal detective stories, "Murders of the Rue Morgue" and "The Purloined Letter." The genre has been launched.

2. Ratiocination and scientism characterize Poe's detective fiction, and we see here the desire for a world that is utterly transparent to the highly intelligent detective, a world where "details" become "clues." From here to Sherlock Holmes and Agatha Christie is a clear route.

C. Science fiction is also one of Poe's "inventions." A number of his stories involve (bogus) scientific discoveries (trips into space, under the seas) that will be played out more fully in the future: Jules Verne, Ray Bradbury, etc.

D. Although he was a poet, Poe gives us, in some stories, a blueprint for urban sociology. His tale "The Man of the Crowd" sketches an entire theory of crowd mentality, and this piece figures profoundly in the poems and prose of Baudelaire.

E. Poe's greatest achievement lies in the area of psychological narrative. In writing his remarkable horror stories, Poe touches on nerves that still quiver today, and our purpose is to examine this body of work.

F. Poe is the man most responsible for today's horror films. Those ghoulish confections with Vincent Price, Peter Cushing, et al, are proof that he is alive and well.

G. Poe is our first literary critic of stature, and he passes (often severe) judgment on the literary performances of his time in the form of articles and essays. His views were astonishingly on target.

V. Poe, jingle-man and analyst, seer and maker, warrants a more careful look.

    A. "Annabel Lee" is one of Poe's most lovely creations, stirring the minds of subsequent writers such as Nabokov, evoking a tragic past.

        1. As usual, Poe gives us beautiful sounds, a hypnotic assemblage of words and rhythms.

        2. Once again, we see Poe's only story: the death of a beautiful woman, located now in some mythic past that we are all invited to share.

        3. Poe's own past is obviously behind this haunting lyric.

        4. "Our" past is perhaps what is ultimately at stake here: if we have grown up with Poe, if we have ever read these pieces at an earlier moment, then they start to "play" again in some strange fashion.

    B. Poe is the great writer of the American collective unconscious: reading him entails digging in our own cellars, which is a central activity in a number of his pieces.

Lecture Ten—Transcript
Edgar Allan Poe

This is Lecture Ten, and it's going to be the first of three lectures on Edgar Allan Poe. I may have taken something of a chance in putting three lectures on Poe in this course. Poe is arguably the most maligned figure in the American canon. I think everybody knows about him, I don't think many people really like to read him very much, anymore. The French are crazy about Poe. Edgar Poe, they think, is their own creation. They also like Jerry Lewis—they have some funny tastes.

In any event, Poe's reputation is perhaps better known than Poe's work. I mean, he is thought to have been the man whom we see in the stories: drunk, sick, kinky, diseased, pervert, necrophiliac, gambler, and a vampire. These are all things that happen in the stories. I think you have to deal with the reputation and, in the first lecture that I'm going to give now, I'm going to talk about the reputation, and I'll talk about the poems briefly. The remaining two lectures will be focused, essentially, on the short stories, the horror stories, because I think that's the genre that Poe is perhaps most remembered for—although his range is much wider than people usually know.

The biography is interesting; Charles Dickens could've imagined his life. He looks a bit like Oliver Twist, or some of the kind of Romantic figures that we see in 19th century literature. He was born in 1809 as the son of traveling actors, and his father abandoned his mother immediately after his birth. The father dies in 1811, and the mother, who is a very talented English actress, soon dies later of consumption. Poe is taken into the home of John and Francis Allan, in Virginia, which is how he becomes Edgar Allan Poe. However, it's important to realize that the Allans' do not adopt him, and his relationship with John Allan is going to remain problematic for all of his life, and have a great impact on his life.

His early schooling is in both Virginia and in England. He was, surprisingly enough, a good athlete. We think of him as this sickly figure. He went to the University of Virginia, and had a notoriously wild life—although that's been exaggerated—a lot of drinking and gambling. It's been exaggerated partly because of the things that happen in the stories, which people take to be verbatim accounts of his life. He has, early on, a failed loved affair with a woman that he then, at the end of his life, does come back to and marry in the last year of his life. In 1829, Mrs. Allan, whom he's very close to, dies of consumption. Poe runs away and joins the army, where he does very well. This too, is counter to our notion of this man. He does well, and in fact, with the help of Allan, is able to get himself admitted to West Point. He is one of the only important American authors to have had that background. We think, in fact, he would've done well at West Point, but Allan refused to continue to fund him. He got himself expelled from West Point, but many people think he did it intentionally. He didn't have any money. He couldn't maintain the position or role that he was in at West Point.

He starts to publish poetry and stories. In 1836, he marries his 14-year old cousin, Virginia Clemm, lived with her, people say, quotes, as "brother and sister." There's a very longstanding theory in literary circles that Poe was either impotent or that this remained a platonic relationship. He's not here to tell us, nor is she. He had a serious career as an editor, as a poet, and as a critic. When he published "The Raven" in 1845, he became famous in America. Virginia, the child bride, his cousin, dies of consumption in 1846. The three ladies, Mom, Mrs. Allan, Virginia, all die of consumption, all the same way. Don't be surprised if the death of women is going to be the central theme in Poe's work. It's the central theme in his life.

Poe comes to us as a man with terrible life habits: drinking, gambling, carousing, and going on binges and sprees—which he did. We also know that he had a very, very bad tolerance for alcohol. He probably didn't consume that much, but it didn't take much to throw him over the edge. He has trouble after the death of Virginia. He goes on more binges and sprees, and he is found finally, semi-conscious, on a Baltimore street in 1849, and is taken to the hospital and dies. It's a kind of meteoric career, of sorts. He was a strange man, a man of impeccable manners—when sober. He is from the Southern culture, an older kind of culture for American writers, courtesy. He was very hard to get on with. Everybody who dealt with him, tangled with him, in some fashion. He seems to have been very finicky. He managed to alienate a lot of people. He was very severe, harsh, unremitting in his judgments, which often turn out to have been very, very good judgments about writers and about things in American culture.

He has been maligned—sort of consistently—by other writers. Emerson referred to him, rather famously as the "jingle man," not a very attractive remark. James Russell Lowell, in a poem that was well-known in the 19th century, said, "Here comes Poe with his raven, like Barnaby Rudge—three-fifths of him genius, two-fifths sheer fudge." This too, helped establish the notion of Poe as not quite serious. Walt Whitman, who's got to be Poe's exact counterpoint, his opposite number, the man who seems to be at the other end of the spectrum, understood Poe's work. He was the only American writer of any importance who came to the Poe memorial in Baltimore. He wrote this about Poe: "Almost without the first sign of moral principle, of the concrete, or of its heroisms, or of the simpler affections of the heart," (These are all the things Poe doesn't have.) "Poe's verses illustrate an intense faculty for technical and abstract beauty, with the rhyming art to excess," (True enough.) "an incurable propensity toward nocturnal themes," (Right on the money, nocturnal themes in Poe.) "a demonical undertone behind every page," (True.) "And, by final judgment, probably," (And here comes Whitman's wonderful image.) "among the electric lights of imaginative literature, brilliant and dazzling, but with no heat." Whitman simply is uncanny.

Other people were less generous. Here's what Henry James said, "It seems to us that to take him with more than a certain degree of seriousness, is to lack seriousness, oneself." And T.S. Eliot goes further: "That Poe had a powerful intellect is undeniable, but it seems to me, the intellect of a highly gifted young person before puberty." He goes on to explain that. "So, what kind of a writer is this guy, the "jingle man?"

I want you to hear some of the jingles. The most famous jingle, is a poem that is appropriately called "The Bells." It spells out Poe, you've got to hear it. Reading it is one thing. Here's how it starts:

> Hear the sledges with the bells -
>
> Silver bells!
>
> What a world of merriment their melody foretells!
>
> How they tinkle, tinkle, tinkle,
>
> In the icy air of night!
>
> While the stars that oversprinkle

All the heavens, seem to twinkle

With a crystalline delight;

Keeping time, time, time,

In a sort of Runic rhyme,

To the tintinnabulation that so musically wells

From the bells, bells, bells, bells,

Bells, bells, bells –

From the jingling and the tinkling of the bells.

And it goes on for stanzas like that. He obviously is trying to replicate the very sound of the bells. I read it to you, because I want you to hear the maniacal repetition in Poe's work, the obsessive repetition of sounds. Poe, more than any writer I know, has thought about what repetition entails. It's a formal way of shaping things. You take sounds and repeat them. That's what poetry consists of—at least, that's what traditional poetry consists of. A rhyme is a repeating sound. But, repetition, what does it mean in the psyche? We know for example, that if we repeat a word very many times to ourselves, it stops having a meaning. If we are obliged to continue to repeat things, it also begins to look like a kind of obsession. I think Poe understands something of the pathological dimensions of repetition. I'll come back to that.

I think one of Poe's most beautiful poems is a poem called, "Eldorado," and it captures a lot of the romanticism of Poe. This is a poem that looks like it comes right out of the Middle Ages. The Middle Ages wouldn't have written it, but it has the motifs of the chivalric age, of the Arthurian period. It's called "Eldorado":

Gaily bedight,

A gallant knight,

In sunshine and in shadow,

Had journeyed long,

Singing a song,

In search of Eldorado.

But he grew old-

This knight so bold-

And o'er his heart a shadow

Fell as he found

No spot of ground

That looked like Eldorado.

And, as his strength

Failed him at length,

He met a pilgrim shadow-

"Shadow," said he,

"Where can it be-

This land of Eldorado?"

"Over the Mountains

Of the Moon,

Down the Valley of the Shadow,

Ride, boldly ride,"

The shadow replied-

"If you seek for Eldorado!"

For my money, there's something haunting that captures you in it. And, when you think that Poe wrote this poem precisely at the moment of the California Gold Rush, so that the search for Eldorado has its very real, cultural, social counterpart, then I think the poem has an even added resonance. What Poe has done is written a poem about "Quest." He's located it back in the chivalric period of the Middle Ages, with the knights searching for Eldorado—the land of gold. I think he's given the measure. Where did people go when they went to the Gold Rush? You can say, "Well, we know where they went. They went to California." No! They didn't go to California. They went where Poe's talking about. They went in search of the absolute. They were on a quest. They were on the kind of journey that Poe has effectively charted here.

Poe's Romanticism is paying its way in this piece. He is, in fact, giving us the measure of the kind of extraordinary appetites and hopes and fantasies that were involved in the California Gold Rush. So, this is again, the kind of testimony that art often gives us, where frequently the sociological or historical record is thin. It doesn't take the measure of what happened.

His most famous poem, as I've said, is "The Raven." Everybody has grown up with "The Raven." Most people have never returned to it, after that. You're going to hear it now—at least a piece of it. Listen to the maniacal repetitions, and the internal rhyming.

> Once upon a midnight dreary, while I pondered, weak and weary,
>
> Over many a quaint and curious volume of forgotten lore,
>
> While I nodded, nearly napping, suddenly there came a tapping,
>
> As of someone gently rapping, rapping at my chamber door.
>
> "Tis some visitor," I muttered, "tapping at my chamber door-
>
> Only this, and nothing more."

This is the voice of a student who is being up late at night, working, and he hears this noise. We have to understand the student has his own particular emotional problems.

> Ah, distinctly I remember it was in the bleak December,
>
> And each separate dying ember wrought its ghost upon the floor.
>
> Eagerly I wished the morrow; —vainly I had sought to borrow
>
> From my books surcease of sorrow—sorrow for the lost Lenore—
>
> For the rare and radiant maiden whom the angels name Lenore—
>
> Nameless here for evermore.

So, here is the young student who is still lamenting the loss of his loved one, Lenore. The whole poem is going to be located in that. It is not Lenore who comes to visit him, but you know who.

Open here I flung the shutter, when, with many a flirt and flutter,

In there stepped a stately raven of the saintly days of yore;

Not the least obeisance made he; not a minute stopped or stayed he;

But, with mien of lord or lady, (I mean, it really gets bad here.) perched above my chamber door- (etcetera)

There is the raven. Now, we all know that this raven has a very peculiar habit of speaking for the poem, which is very, very natural for a parrot, for example. The raven knows only one word, and we know what that word is, "Nevermore." It's going to be perfectly positioned in this poem. That's the one word that's going to catalyze everything else. For the student who is moaning, or bemoaning the loss of his loved one, "Nevermore" starts to fill in that emotional blank. So the student gets increasingly worked up.

"Prophet!" said I, "thing of evil—prophet still, if bird or devil!

By that Heaven that bends above us—by that God we both adore—

Tell this soul with sorrow laden if, within the distant Aidenn,

It shall clasp a sainted maiden whom the angels name Lenore—

Clasp a rare and radiant maiden whom the angels name Lenore."

Quoth the Raven, "Nevermore."

And so the poem closes on that note, as the speaker gets more and more fiendishly worked up.

"Be that word our sign in parting, bird or fiend," I shrieked, upstarting—

"Get thee back into the tempest and the Night's Plutonian shore!

Leave no black plume as a token of that lie thy soul hath spoken!

Leave my loneliness unbroken! — quit the bust above my door!

Take thy beak from out my heart, and take thy form from off my door!"]

(Etcetera, the constant refrain.)

Quote the raven, "Nevermore."

The last stanza says that the raven's still there. The raven, never flitting, *still* is sitting, *still* is sitting on the pallid bust of Pallas, just above my chamber door. We'll close, you know, with "Nevermore."

Now this is the poem, as I said, that was the most famous one that he wrote. Poe himself, in an essay that I'm going to refer to later, talked about this poem, and he explained that it's a very carefully worked out poem. He takes the natural fact that the bird can only speak one sound, and he works it into a kind of crescendo of effects with the situation, nightmarish effects, really. It is a kind of philosophy of doom, really, with the student in the room. So the repetition, "Nevermore," "Nevermore," "Nevermore," once again starts to become wildly significant.

Poe, was a figure who had a certain reputation in the United States. As I said, people read "The Raven." But in fact, what happened to Poe is that some of his work was seen by some of the major French writers, and that's what changed everything. In particular, he wrote an essay the year after "The Raven," called "The Philosophy of Composition," or another title is more direct, "How I Wrote The Raven" is what he called it also. Particularly, Baudelaire read this piece—and I'll talk about that in a minute. It's astonishing. It's a key moment in the evolution of thinking about literature in the 19th century.

What Poe says in this essay, "How I Wrote The Raven," is what I was alluding to just a moment ago, which is that every effect in this poem is calculated and planned. There is nothing of inspiration. There's nothing spontaneous in this poem. Moreover, Poe goes on to say there never has been anything spontaneous in poetry. Poe is making a huge statement here. That whole notion of the poet, as somehow inspired by the muse, which we have all the way from classical antiquity, Poe says, "No, no. That's an illusion. Poets are people who sit down with rhyme schemes, metric arrangements, with a plan, and they work out every effect that they achieve."

He says that the joke is, that no one has written about that yet, and "I'm now going to do it." What you have here is a cashiering of the whole Romantic notion of poetry as the divine inspiration of the poet, who was you know, in the ecstatic mood because the gods are speaking to him. Instead, you've got the poet as craftsman, poet as seer, poet as artisan, and poet as a person who's a word-maker. It had nothing to do with great visions. It's nothing to do with being inspired. It has to do with a very strategic way, a tactical way, of using language. Every effect is planned, as I said. So that's what he goes on to show you: exactly how he wrote "The Raven."

There was everything in it. First of all, he tells you in this essay what his major goals are. What is the major province of poetry? For Poe, it's simple beauty. Beauty is the sole legitimate province of poetry. What's the right tone for poetry? Poe loves to legislate. "The right tone of poetry is sadness. Melancholy is thus the most legitimate of all poetical tones." If you've got beauty as the subject, and melancholy as the tone, what would be the most perfect topic? "Of all melancholy topics," Poe says, "what is the most melancholy?" Death was the obvious. Okay, what kind of death? The death of a beautiful woman! Perfect, you have it. It fills exactly what the theory says. It just also happens to be the fact of the man's life.

I want you to see this, that on the one hand, he is giving us a very, very savvy theory about why he puts into his poems what he does, and on the other hand—the hand that the French did not know anything about—he's coming to this, out of his own compulsions, out of the fateful events of his upbringing, and of his life. He has some wonderful things in this essay. He explains about refrain; that refrain is a critical part, again, of the repeating dimensions of poetry. The refrain has to have a key word that has to be used over and over. He said, "It's obvious, scientifically obvious, that the right way to do this is to use the long-O as the most sonorous vowel, in connection with the R, as the most producible consonant." Oh! So that's the science of that.

Needless to say, if you are working with a long O, and an R, it would've been impossible. As Poe writes, "In such a search, it would've been absolutely impossible to overlook the word 'Nevermore.' In fact, it was the very first which presented itself," he said. Did it, Mr. Poe? That's right? Okay, so "nevermore" is how this is going to work. He gives you this incredible explanation of how everything in this poem "The Raven" has been planned in advance, a seminar on how to construct a poem. The French took him totally at his word. The French term for this is *boutade,* which means it's a joke, it's a spoof, or it's a setup. It's true in part, and it covers up a lot of stuff, too. The French loved it. In a sense, if they got it wrong, it doesn't make any difference, because they did what they did with this essay, and because Baudelaire, who was a much greater poet than Poe, writes poems along the lines of Poe's reasoning here.

That this thing enters literary history, and changes—marks the death knell of a certain kind of Romanticism. In fact, you have a view of poetry as craft, as constructed, as strategic, as anti-Romantic, anti-inspirational, and Baudelaire has wonderful lines about this. Baudelaire, appropriately then, moves. He doesn't write about ravens. He writes about walking in the cities and things like that, more modern, contemporary subjects, but he is using Poe's model. It's not just Baudelaire. He champions Poe. He translates Poe. The example of Poe is the central one, it seems to me, in his own poetic practice.

He then, goes on to influence several generations of great French writers, in particular, Stephané Mallarmé, who is a very, very great poet, and closer to Poe, in many ways, than Baudelaire. There is Paul Valéry—and the joke here is that Eliot, who has claimed that Poe is the person that has the intelligence of a young person before puberty—absorbs huge doses of Poe by reading Baudelaire, and Valéry, and all these other people.

Poe is in the bloodstream. You can like him, or dislike him, and you can claim it's pre-puberty, but he's there. Therefore, I want to say, that in some ways, he is the most influential—hear me, not the best—the most influential American man of letters in the 19th century. He gets everywhere. He takes this trip through Western poetry and changes things. I've just suggested one way in which that's the case, which is that he helps to shape the course of modern poetry, but that's not all, and here's where I want to focus on my assertion that Poe's work is much more varied than we might think.

Poe essentially invents the detective story—invents it. He creates this man, Dupont. He writes three detective stories, two of which are extraordinarily famous: "The Murders in the Rue Morgue" and "The

Purloined Letter," which people are still writing about. It's engaged the most interesting psychoanalytic thinkers of the time. Jacques Lacan, the great guru of French linguistic psychoanalysis, has written a very famous essay on "The Purloined Letter" as being a kind of allegory of the status of language and the unconscious. It's a brilliant essay. The fact is that Poe writes the detective story, and in it, he expresses all of his own belief, or his desire to believe in rationalization, in reason, in the world being reducible to analytic process and analytic powers. It's the great scientific side of Poe.

Again, it's consistent with that essay, against inspiration. Poe wants the world to become transparent to the man of strong intellectual powers. Now, the detective's story's going to have a huge vogue, but at its core, the detective is the person for whom all things that look like details for you, become clues for him. That everything shows its cogency—shows its part, its role—in the larger design. You can see that. We don't read Poe, but we've all read Sherlock Holmes. We've read Agatha Christie. It's the same model. Poe proceeds the same way. You look at a situation, and you see the things that others have missed, and you know how to properly put them in the right place. Poe starts this. You can almost bring this back to Emerson. This is a sense of self-reliance. The individual mind is capable of taking the world of discreet phenomena and seeing the kind of mosaic that they belong to when put together in the right way.

That's just one side of Poe. Allied to that is that Poe is also the genesis of science fiction. In some of his stories, like "The Balloon-Hoax" or "Descent into the Maelstrom," Poe writes things that lead directly to Jules Verne, and then to Ray Bradbury, and then to all of our own 20th century kinds of science fiction writers, that he takes this rational process and extends it into the elements, into the heavens, and into the oceans. In many cases, some of his stories were thought to be actual scientific experiments. They didn't know that this was just literature.

Here, I'm going to make a different kind of argument. He creates a kind of literature that is close to urban sociology. One of his most interesting stories is called, "The Man of the Crowd." And it's a story that's very seminal, because Baudelaire, who loved Poe, loved that piece and did more with it than Poe did, and did different things with it. It's one of the first pieces we have about the reality of crowds as being one of the key facts of city life. A crowd has a very funny kind of behavior, which you couldn't have talked about if you lived in a rural [area.] That's not something that Coleridge is going to be able to talk about, if you're writing about life, and nature, and life in the woods. It's something that Emerson and Thoreau didn't touch. But Poe does, and he talks about a new kind of mentality. It's kind of a strange tale, about a person who really comes to life by dint of the intensity and vibrancy of city crowds.

This is a figure who follows crowds all day long, in London, which is where the story is set. It's an interesting notion of a new species, a kind of urban species that is not motivated in the same way that earlier kinds of social groups were. I think his greatest contribution, and it's where most of these lectures are going to be, is in the realm of psychological narrative—horror stories—but as psychological narrative, and those are the ones that I'm going to talk about. That's the legacy. That's where he's with us. As one critic said, "He is the unpaid script writer of films by Roger Corman, Freddie Frances, Vincent Price, Christopher Lee, Peter Cushing, *Friday the 13th*, all of the stuff that the young people have been watching for the last 10 or 20 years, Edgar Poe is there." He's the guy who gave the idea for most of those stories. The horror tradition, which we may want to think that this isn't serious literature, is certainly serious money. It's certainly serious film. It's certainly serious cartoons. Poe is more alive than ever, in that arena, and I will want to talk about that.

One final thing about Poe, and I'm going to return to his poetry. He's also our first, major literary critic. He pronounced judgment on all of the major writers of the 19th century, and his judgment, as I said, was austere—but pretty much on the money. There's a kind of professionalism, a kind of sense of standards in Poe's critical work that is a model. I want to return to the "jingle man." I'm going to read what I think of as, in a sense, his most perfect poem, and it's called "Annabel Lee."

> It was many and many a year ago,
>
> In a kingdom by the sea
>
> That a maiden there lived whom you may know
>
> By the name of Annabel Lee;
>
> And this maiden she lived with no other thought
>
> Than to love and be loved by me.

I was a child and she was a child,

In this kingdom by the sea,

But we loved with a love that was more than love-

I and my Annabel Lee-

With a love that the winged seraphs of heaven

Coveted her and me.

And this was the reason that, long ago,

In this kingdom by the sea,

A wind blew out of a cloud, chilling

My beautiful Annabel Lee;

So that her high-born kinsman came

And bore her away from me,

To shut her up in a sepulchre

In this kingdom by the sea.

The angels, not half so happy in heaven,

Went envying her and me-

Yes!- that was the reason (as all men know,

In this kingdom by the sea)

That the wind came out of the cloud by night,

Chilling and killing my Annabel Lee.

That's tuberculosis, "chilling and killing my Annabel Lee."

But our love it was stronger by far than the love

Of those who were older than we-

Of many far wiser than we-

And neither the angels in heaven above,

Nor the demons down under the sea,

Can ever dissever my soul from the soul

Of the beautiful Annabel Lee:

For the moon never beams, without bringing me dreams

Of the beautiful Annabel Lee,

And the stars never rise, but I feel the bright eyes

Of the beautiful Annabel Lee:

And so, all the night-tide, I lie down by the side

Of my darling- my darling- my life and my bride,

In the sepulcher there by the sea-

In her tomb by the sounding sea.

It's a hypnotic poem. It's got all of Poe's cadences. It's got all of the repetitions and the rhymes. It's got all of Poe. It's the death of the beautiful woman. It's the childhood moment when psyche is formed, children loving one another. It's the child bride, if you want. It's also the fact that she is still alive for him, although she is dead. It closes with a moment of entering into the tomb, being buried alive. It's going to be the central theme in Poe's work. All of Poe's phantasms are beautifully coded together in this piece. It all still lives—everything speaks of this woman—the stars. "The moon never beams without bringing me dreams." Everything. "The stars never rise, but I feel her bright eyes." The universe writes large, our psyche. The universe reflects the inner world.

Part of my reason for doing Poe is that Poe is "there." He's not just there in the world of influencing 19th century literature, and he's not just there in horror films. He's "there," it seems to me, in the substratum of everybody's psyche in this country. We've all had our little dosage of Poe. We've read him when we were young. And, when I was young, my father—who had only had a high school education and did not, in fact, much care for literature—in his 60s and 70s, would recite this poem, "Annabel Lee." I remember hearing him, when I was still young, talk about this poem. He could cite the whole thing from beginning to end, and I never thought much about what that poem meant, or what it meant for him to be doing it, until I returned to Poe and realized Poe exists there. He's there, humming on the bottoms of our minds, and we need to bring him up, and take a look.

Lecture Eleven
Poe—Ghost Writer

Scope:

Well before Robert Louis Stevenson's "Dr. Jekyll and Mr. Hyde," Poe gave us the story of the divided self. In his most famous version of psychological doubling, "William Wilson," Poe recasts (in darker versions) a number of events from his own past and suggests that all lives are haunted by ghosts of our own making, notably a conscience and consciousness that we cannot silence. The more famous version of "killing one's double" occurs in "The Cask of Amontillado," in which many of Poe's phantasms—being buried alive, murdering without detection, the sweetness of revenge—are on show. Our brief look at the little-known story "The Facts in the Case of M. Valdemar" will focus on the mind/body dichotomy in Poe. Then we will close with an analysis of the quintessential horror story, "The Fall of the House of Usher," now seen as allegory of the divided psyche torn by love and hate.

Objectives: Upon completion of this lecture, you should be able to:

1. Summarize the role of the doppelgänger in "William Wilson."

2. Explain how Roderick Usher embodies the artist in "The Fall of the House of Usher."

3. Describe the role of empiricism in Poe's narrative strategy.

Outline

I. Poe's stories, like his poems, rehearse the key events of his life and make us understand the "inner wiring" that is never visible in people but that governs their lives nonetheless.

    A. "William Wilson" is Poe's classic version of the doppelgänger motif, the unsettling appearance of a "double" or "twin" who is/is not you.

        1. Poe's life, made worse, appears in this tale: in the figure of Wilson the narrator, we see the gambling, the drinking, the excesses that Poe knew all too well.

        2. Poe's story centers, however, on the entry of Wilson #2, the rival, the double, yet we do not know if this figure is visible to others or not.

3. Being "twinned" to Wilson is the narrator's chief burden, and in the Siamese-twin relationship we see an unmistakable parable about conscience that haunts us.

4. Wilson #2 is quickly identified with the keener moral sense, the judgment that is relentlessly (and ceaselessly) passed on our misdeeds.

5. The narrator expresses a nagging sense of prior oneness with Wilson #2, as if they were sundered only by the accident of birth, suggesting a virtually platonic model of the divided psyche at last united.

6. The narrator's evil career—gambling, cheating, robbing, and seducing—reads like a nightmarish account of Poe's own life—yet, he is everywhere tracked by Wilson #2.

7. The story heats up because of Wilson #2's increased agency, his willingness to speak out and to expose the narrator's crimes.

8. The narrator's trajectory becomes wilder and wilder, international in circuit, right up to the final, fateful encounter with Wilson #2.

9. Poe's parable differs from the story of Jekyll and Hyde, in which innocence remains the vantage point. Instead, we see a different set of actions altogether—do evil and judge your self. With this punitive model of consciousness, Freud is in sight.

B. "The Cask of Amontillado" is one of Poe's most famous stories about doing in doubles, about the pleasures of murder.

1. Motivation is a mystery in this piece, which leads the reader to ponder still further the rationale of this ritualistic murder.

2. Poe's classic setting in the catacombs suggests that our deepest drives bring us closer and closer to the land of the dead, a place that seems central to Poe's topography.

3. Poe's verbal conceits are riddles as well in this piece, as if the narrator wanted to celebrate the double-ness of language as well as of identity.

4. One feels that there is a fated unity in this piece between the killer and his victim. Consider the two names: Fortunato and Montresor, each revolving around the concept of "treasure," each a version of the other. Poe

seems to be wrestling with the riddle of identity, as if identity itself were a wrestling match or a duel.

5. The beautifully executed murder in this story obliges us to think symbolically, to see this conflict as mind vs. body. There is no mere killing here, but rather a burial of one's enemy alive, and we need to ponder the difference, the kind of "benefit" the narrator derives from such acts.

6. Poe's story illustrates the civil war in the mind; but, as usual, he goes all the way, beyond conflict to resolution. Yet, because this story is told 50 years after the events take place, we may wonder whether there is any closure or not.

II. Disciplining the body seems to be a major concern in Poe, especially if we consider "Amontillado" as a punishment of the physical self.

A. "The Facts in the Case of M. Valdemar" is one of Poe's least known but grisliest stories, focused entirely on the body/mind dichotomy, but cued even more sharply to issues of "voice."

1. Poe refers to mesmerism at the tale's beginning, and we need to recover something of the prestige and fascination of this concept in the 19th century.

2. "Facts" is the word used in Poe's title, and when we reflect that this tale was originally taken to be a true scientific experiment, the line between fact and fiction grows dim.

3. Poe's empiricism is startling in this piece; unlike the customary Romantic idiom in most of his pieces, Poe describes the human body with morbid realistic detail.

4. The story enacts a strange triumph of the spirit: a voice emerges from the tomb.

5. Poe's story of a dead body speaking is at the outer limit of his war between mind and body. It is the allegory of art, art now understood as an imperishable voice, unlike the one-time body that housed it. It is also a parable of lectures-on-tape, of the electronic miracle that transcends time and flesh.

6. Poe is sufficiently tough-minded to ask: Can this be done? His grisly finish depicts, in all its horror, the scandal of flesh.

B. Poe's gambit, much like Emily Dickinson's, is to speak from uninhabitable places.

III. "The Fall of the House of Usher" is usually seen as Poe's masterpiece, and its impact on other writers is traceable.

A. The macabre setting of the story—the decaying ancestral house, the fungi—seems to be a setting of the soul. Could this be a metaphor for the dead South?

B. The story comes into being because of Usher's call for help; that is why the narrator comes, and it suggests a link between Usher and narrator that is symbolic as well.

   1. Usher is presented as end-of-the-line, as last descendent of a genteel family; Poe seems to be speaking here about sterility vs. creativity.

   2. Usher's strange sister triangulates Poe's arrangements here—the dying Madeline is Usher's "complement" just as Usher "completes" the narrator.

C. Usher is, interestingly, the artist as well, so that this story sheds light on artistic practice, too.

   1. In the brief descriptions of Usher's work, we get a precocious picture of a kind of painting that will become, a century later, abstract art.

   2. Madeline's dying serves, tragically, as Usher's source of power; her process of dying seems to animate his work.

   3. Dying—not death, but dying—may thus be thought of as the generator of Poe's art, life, and stories are out to trace this trajectory, to suck all possible energy out of it.

   4. When Usher acknowledges that he has put Madeline, living, into the tomb, he reveals the deepest wellsprings of his own modus operandi.

   5. Murdering one's beloved/double is increasingly coming into focus as Poe's view of our internal wiring. Do we write off this philosophy as simply gibberish and sensational, or does it have its ugly truth?

Lecture Eleven—Transcript
Poe—Ghost Writer

This is Lecture Eleven, and it's the second of my three lectures on Edgar Allan Poe. This, and the next one, are both going to focus on Poe's short stories because I think that they are really representative of his most pithy, virulent work. Those are also the stories that probably are most powerfully lodged in our collective subconscious. I'll want to try to get at that. The kinds of stories that I'm going to talk about today are, for the most part, dealing with the issue of "the double." If you'll allow me, I'd like to suggest that the double in a kind of psychological sense is not unrelated to the repetition device in the poems.

Poe is struck by analogy, he's struck by kinship, he's struck by likeness, and he's going to insist on these characteristics in circumstances where we don't anticipate them. It's in that sense that these pieces have a kind of family resemblance. The most explicit one is Poe's story, "William Wilson," which is not known by everybody, but the Poe buffs like it a great deal. Then I'll also talk about one of his most achieved short pieces, "The Cask of Amontillado," which I take to be one of his funniest stories—if Poe could be funny. Then, I will take a piece that no one knows, "The Facts in the Case of M. Valdemar." I'll close with some remarks on what is conceivably his most famous story, certainly his most baroque story, which is, "The Fall of the House of Usher." That is a lot to do!

It's the case that a number of the misconceptions or the exaggerated notions that we have of Poe's life come from the story, "William Wilson," because in large measure, "William Wilson" rewrites the biography, but it rewrites it on a darker plain. It, in fact, brands the protagonist with activities that Poe probably was <u>not</u> guilty of. This figure also leads a wild life as a student, but this figure gambles and cheats. We don't have any reason to think that Poe ever cheated. Poe was still bound by a kind of honor code in his own life, but, for some reason—and it's worth pondering over what the reason would be—recasts himself in even more diabolic forms in his short stories.

This is a story of a character that calls himself William Wilson. We know that's not his real name. He calls himself William Wilson, and he talks about his background. He went to school in England. He was involved in gambling. We watch this story develop the life, really, of a fairly considerable villain who acknowledges it. There's no bones made about it. He starts out dissolute and gambling, and then he moves on to seduction, to cheating and, finally, to murder. All of this is delivered with a certain amount of bravado, and it's also part of the kind of arrogance of this character, because the dominant trait of Wilson is that other people cannot ever challenge his willpower. Now, what is interesting about this story—and the reason that I'm giving it to us at this point—is that his life is consistently interrupted by another figure, which becomes his rival. Would you believe that this other figure's name is William Wilson? That's what his name is, even though they are pseudonyms. So, we're definitely not only dealing with doubles, we're dealing with a sense, that in the school situation where this strange person appears, nobody else seems to pay much attention.

The protagonist talks about his own strength over the others, his ascendancy over all of his peers with one exception, "which was found in the person or a scholar who, although no relation, bore the same Christian and surname as myself." This is the one figure who will not knuckle under, bow down, to the protagonist's ambitions. He goes on to claim that, "Strangely enough, the two of us were born on the same day." And what an odd coincidence that would be, too. He says, "This was not acknowledged by anyone but myself." It's also the case that, as I said, that the newcomer Wilson—Wilson #2, we can call him—consistently challenges the narrator. That's important because he's a thorn in his side. We realize that there's obviously a kind of emerging "twinship" in this story and that it's carried out on a number of different levels.

One of the important levels is voice. The narrator talks about his own voice, and he talks about the fact that Wilson comes in with the same kind of voice, but a slightly lower version of it, a very low whisper, and, "A singular whisper, it grew to be a very clear echo of my own." You can tell that he's being increasingly galled by the presence of this strange look-alike, sound alike, double, which is there. We learn that there are some key differences between them. Not only does Wilson #2 challenge the speaker, but Wilson #2 is also endowed with a moral sense, according to the speaker, that is "far keener than my own." In a very interesting notation, the narrator says, "That I could with difficulty shake off the belief of my having been acquainted with the being who stood before me at some epic very long ago, at some point of the past, even infinitely remote, as if we were somehow joined long ago."

You almost get the sense that this is a platonic allegory or a fable of the soul. In this case, it would be two parts that were at some earlier time, some perhaps primeval time, linked together in unity and that now are split, fissured, and that that's the story Poe's trying to tell. Wilson #2 is the second half, the kind of severed Siamese twin who's going to come in and make his presence known. He's the angelic half. He's the keener moral sense, and he's the one who upbraids this villainous narrator.

Well, the story proceeds apace. This fellow does all the things that we know that Poe did. He gets himself kicked out of various schools. As I said, he's one notch darker than anything Poe achieved. In the story, he drinks, he gambles, and he goes from Eton to Oxford. He cheats at cards at Oxford. It's a portrait of deception. In a key moment, right when he is getting ready to take advantage of this very wealthy student at Oxford, Glenn Denning, in comes you know who—
Wilson #2. This nagging conscience comes in and has something to say to the group of people right at the moment when the protagonist is going to really clean up with all the cheating.

> "Gentlemen," he said in a low, distinct, and never-to-be-forgotten whisper which thrilled to the very marrow of my bones, "Gentlemen, I make no apology for this behavior, because in thus behaving, I am but fulfilling a duty. You are, beyond doubt, uninformed of the true character of the person who has to-night won at *écarté* a large sum of money from Lord Glendenning. I will therefore put you upon an expeditious and decisive plan of obtaining this very necessary information. Please to examine, at your leisure, the inner linings of the cuff of his left sleeve, and the several little packages which may be found in the somewhat capacious pockets of his embroidered morning wrapper."

Wilson #2 exposes the cheat. This is the kind of clear pattern of the story. That right before he can make his killing, as it were, he is going to be exposed by this nagging but relentless figure, which seems to appear out of nowhere. We then follow the protagonist further. He's kicked out of Oxford. That doesn't stop him in his international career. He goes on to Rome, to Vienna, to Berlin, to Moscow. The final encounter is at a masked ball in Rome where our protagonist is hungrily preparing another coup. This time, he's going to seduce this woman who's the wife of a friend and he's getting all set for it. (It's a masked ball, as I said.) Needless to say, he is going to be tapped on the shoulder by some new person, who isn't new to us.

"I felt a light hand placed on my shoulder and that ever-remembered low, damnable whisper within my ear." And he looks at this person and this person is wearing a cloak of blue velvet. "'Scoundrel!' I said in a voice husky with rage, while every syllable I uttered seemed as new fuel to my fury. 'Scoundrel! Imposter!'" It's a good word for this story. "Imposter, a cursed villain. You shall not dog me unto death! Follow me or I stab you where you stand." And he pulls him into the next room. He drags him in there. Then he thrusts him up against the wall and says, "Now we're going to fight." And the other figure reluctantly goes into the fight. Poe writes:

> The contest was brief indeed. I was frantic with every species of wild excitement, and felt within my single arm the energy and power of a multitude. In a few seconds I forced him by sheer strength against the wainscoting, and thus, getting him at mercy, plunged my sword, with brute ferocity, repeatedly through and through his bosom.

That's one way of getting rid of this guy. How do you imagine this story is going to end? At that instant, some person tries to get into the room. The narrator has to go over and go back to the door. He turns around. "But what human language can adequately portray that astonishment, that horror which possessed me at the spectacle then presented to view?" What does he see? He sees that the room has changed. "A large mirror, so at first it seemed to me in my confusion, now stood where none had been perceptible before. And as I stepped up to it in extremity of terror, mine own image, but with features all pale and dabbled in blood, advanced to meet me with a feeble and tottering gait."

We are getting increasingly the explicit message here that Wilson is a figure of himself, but the story consistently wants you to see the two as separate.

Thus it appeared, I say, but was not. It was my antagonist—it was Wilson, who then stood before me in the agonies of his dissolution. His mask and cloak lay, where he had thrown them, upon the floor. Not a thread on his raiment—not a line in all the marked and singular lineaments of his face which was not, even the most absolute identity, mine own!

It was Wilson, but something has changed. He no longer speaks with a whisper. "And instead", the writer says, "I could have fancied it was I myself speaking when he said," and here's the last lines of the story, "You have conquered and I yield. Yet hence forward art thou also dead, dead to the world, to heaven and to hope. In me didst thou exist and in my death see, by this image which is thine own, how utterly thou hast murdered thyself."

It's Poe's story of civil war, if you will, as a kind of psychic civil war. It's the reverse of Stevenson's "Dr. Jekyll and Mr. Hyde." "Dr. Jekyll and Mr. Hyde" is an optimistic story written from the point of view of Dr. Jekyll who has this dark double that he does everything in his power to control. We see a kind of story of Victorian repression in Stevenson's story. However, here, the central figure is Hyde. If you want to go back to Jekyll and Hyde, the apparition would be Jekyll. The real person, the person who is the publicly endorsed figure—and the energized, empowered figure—is going to be Hyde. It's going to be the first William Wilson. This is not a story in which innocence worries about its own potential for violence and butchery. It's rather a story about doing evil and then killing your conscience, if you can. That's going to be a kind of persistent motif in Poe's work, that duel—that fight to the death.

The next story I want to allude to in this regard is one of his most achieved stories. It's "The Cask of Amontillado," and I think it's also a really a delightful story in its own way. It's got a kind of humor that most of Poe doesn't have. It starts with an enigma. We don't ever know why this particular elaborate revenge is happening. It's not motivated. We don't know why. He says, "The thousand injuries of Fortunato I had born as best as I could." We won't know what they are. "But when he ventured upon insult," We don't know what that was either. "I vowed revenge." Okay? What will this revenge be? Well, this is going to be one of the most famous burials in literature and it's done with a certain amount of humor.

How are you going to get Fortunato to come into that place where you're going to bury him? Ah! You tell him, because you know he is a great lover of Amontillado, of fine sherry—a very particular kind of sherry. You tell him that you have gotten hold of a pipe—as they say, of it—that is quite special and that perhaps he's interested.

"My dear Fortunato, you are luckily met. ...I have received a pipe of what passes for Amontillado, and I have my doubts."

"How?" said he, "Amontillado? A pipe? Impossible? And in the middle of a carnival?" (It's a characteristic Poe setting. They're all dressed in costumes and we're going to see that the costume of Fortunato is interesting here.)

"I have my doubts." (In other words, whether this is really the authentic Amontillado.) "And I thought of finding you. But you were not to be found, and I was fearful of losing a bargain."

"Amontillado!"

"I have my doubts."

"Amontillado!"

"And I must satisfy them."

"Amontillado!"

"As you were engaged, I was on my way to Luchesi. If any one has a critical turn, it is he. He will tell me—"

"Luchesi cannot tell Amontillado from Sherry."

So, there's a sense in which this guy is just beautifully sucked in to the drama here, that he's going to bring Fortunato in, and this refrain, this is repetition again—It's not quite poetry, but—"Amontillado? Amontillado?" That's going to be the constant rhyming device within the story. He's going to bring him in, and we watch this increasing form of entrapment in this piece. You see this piece is playful. It's playful, and I chuckle at the way this person is brought in. It's playful with its amount of puns, that they are drinking wine as they walk into this catacomb-like cave or cellar where the speaker, Montresor has his collection. He opens a bottle of wine that's called De Grave. Grave, of course, is a famous Bordeaux area, but of course it means, in English, "grave." There are lots of little puns. It turns out at one point that the one is being taken Fortunato, makes a special sign, and he makes it again, a weird sign, a gesticulation.

"You do not comprehend?" he said.

"Not I," I replied.

"Then you are not of the brotherhood."

"How?"

"You are not of the masons."

(He is talking about the Free Masons.)

"Yes, yes. A mason. Yes, a mason. A sign."

Of course he's going to a very different kind of Mason. He's going to end up using a trowel, and he's going to build a wall, and he's going to seal this guy up for eternity. Poe is having fun with his words either being repeated, being echoed, or being pirouetted. Masons are going to run this story. A "Free Mason" is really what this guy turns out to be. He's going to free himself of Fortunato through his masonry!

I'm calling this story another story of the divided self, and the reason I'm doing that is that the two names of these people are Fortunato and Montresor. These are both puns about treasure and about riches. But the similarity in the two names suggests that they're versions of each other. Therefore, Fortunato, as well, is drunk when the story starts, and he's dressed in fools motley, and he's got the bells on and everything, and it's not hard to see that he could be a kind of foolish—a kind of corporal side of this very sophisticated and suave protagonist. We're not far from William Wilson here. That's what's being "done in." You want to get rid of that side. The insult that presumably starts the story is not really important it seems to me. What you've got is a ritual killing, a ritual civil war. You're going to get rid of your double. You're going to get rid of the person whose name is yours, Fortunato, Montresor, and you're going to do it in such a way that no one can ever catch you at it. That's always the great pleasure in Poe.

You could see it as an allegory of mind versus body, the drunkenness of the person. Fortunato has a terrible cold. There's room in his eyes. You've got a whole line and a half that goes just like, (coughing). It's just "ugh, ugh, ugh" written about 25 times. That's also poetry, if you wish. It's rhyme, rhyme, rhyme, rhyme, rhyme. But it's also the noise of the body that's not speaking. It's just purely phlegmatic. It's clearing its throat, it's coughing. That's the sound that you've got to get rid of. You want the clarity, the purity of brain, of design, of strategy. You want to move this lug. As they say in—you know, about Polonius. "I'll lug the guts in the other room." It's the weighty body that has to be disposed of, and it's going to be disposed of.

At the end of the story, one of the great lines is right before he's completely put away. Poor Fortunato is still saying, "Amontillado?" He hasn't gotten the message. He's a bit drunk at this point as well. Again, there are the same repetitions. "Amontillado? Ah, yeah, Amontillado." And then, "For the love of God!" That's when he finally realizes. "For the love of God, Montresor. Yes, for the love of God." The last sign or sound that we hear is the jingling of the bells, and it reminds me of that poem that I started my Poe lectures with—about "The Bells" poem—that this is a grisly story of murder that has been set to music in some way. It is still seen as a kind of phonic story, and the bells that are on the fool's motley of Fortunato, in some sense, punctuate the story. They are the signs again of the second part of the self as being inferior, of being a fool, of having to be disposed of, but also having its own kind of music. All he hears at the end is a jingling of the bells, and he puts him away.

Then we have this astonishing last line of this story, after he has put the last stone into place and bricked him up. There's always a kind of artistic pleasure in the Poe murdering stories where the murderer does it with such skill and poise and dispatch. It's the same technical prowess that you see in the making of a poem. He puts him away and then he says, "For the half of a century, no mortal has disturbed them. In pace requiescat!" And you realize this thing happened 50 years ago, but it's told as if it were happening right now or yesterday. I think that's not an accident. I think that part of Poe's real concept here is that this is going on over and over and over. This isn't a murder story. I called it that, but that's not true. He doesn't kill him. He simply puts him away. He buries him alive. It's a perfect way of keeping him there. We don't know when Fortunato actually dies. You could claim that he's still alive 50 years later. It's being told 50 years later. This burying alive is a way of keeping the dying permanently expendable. Death doesn't quite happen. This is going to be one of the projects in Poe.

The story reminds me of certain kinds of insect practices where another insect will be caught, but not quite killed, just maybe paralyzed so that the young can feed on this not yet dead body; and so that the body, that's not yet died, furnishes substance for the other. That's the kind of parasitical relationship between the two selves in Poe. You want to do in somebody, but you don't want them to be totally dead and out of the picture. It's the dying itself that's going to furnish you with the sustenance that you need.

Now, I'm going to go quickly to this other weird story. They're all weird, but this one is unknown and that's called, "The Facts in the Case of M. Valdemar." It's a story that is under the sign of mesmerism, and Poe talks about that. Mesmerism is an enormously powerful intellectual movement in the middle and late half of the 19th century. In particular, it has to do with hypnosis, it has to do with séances, it has to do with the belief that spirit outlives matter, that you can call back the dead, and that you can somehow be in touch with the realm of spirits. It's a kind of last-ditch religious rejection of the scientific movement, of the prestige of science, which gives you only a kind of empirical phenomenal world. Mesmerism says, "No, no, no, no. Beyond the material world, beyond the carnal world of the body, there is the soul, and there's spirit." The Mesmerists were not different that much from the alchemists, from people who were talking about what lives behind the world of phenomena.

That's what this text is about. It's about the traffic of spirit. It's about spirit independent of flesh. In particular, it's about the power of hypnosis. So this man, Valdemar, who's dying, is hypnotized at the moment of death and is retained in that state for seven months. That's the project. When this was published, people thought it was a real medical text. They thought it was true. Well, it's a very interesting thing. Through hypnosis, they can make him talk, even though he is probably dead, or he's right at death—a voice from the tomb, right? But you don't even need a tomb here. Hypnosis just does it all for you. He's lying in that bed and they actually bring back his voice, and it's a voice that Poe says that comes from a vast distance, some deep cavern within the earth. It says, "yes," "no," "I have been sleeping, and now I am dead." Of course, we all know, that's the one phrase that we will probably never be able to say, that it's not linguistically—or any other way really—very credible. Yet, that's what this voice says. Seven months they keep him like this.

This text is like a triumph of the spirit. In some ways, it seems to me, that this text, this voice from death—to preserve the voice, to preserve the spirit and the brain from the decay of the body—that is what literature always is. Literature is the voice that outlives the body. Literature is the recorded text, the words on a page that still are real, even though that body decomposed centuries ago. In a sense, this is one of the oldest things we know about literature, that it has that kind of immortality—or can have. What is remarkable in this text is that it's not just the written word it's the spoken word. It's the oral self that is going to perhaps outlive the body. It's not totally fanciful to even connect that with what we're doing here. This lecture, if it is seen at a time when I am dead or whatever, there I am. I'm speaking. I can be seen. I can be heard. Electronically, it's possible to do what this story is talking about, which is to keep a voice alive and perceptible well after its origin—its source—has decomposed. It's exactly what the story does.

What is quite astounding is the way in which this thing closes. Where we realize that you can't beat flesh. You might have tricks up your sleeve to keep voices going, but you can't beat flesh. So, at the end, they try to wake him up. You can imagine what's going to happen.

> As I rapidly made the mesmeric passes, amid ejaculations of 'dead! dead!' absolutely bursting from the tongue and not from the lips of this sufferer, his whole frame at once— within the space of a single minute, or even less, shrunk— crumbled—absolutely *rotted* away beneath my hands. Upon the bed, before the whole company, there lay a nearly liquid mass of loathsome—of detestable putridity.

This is Poe going the absolute full route. This is what the fate of flesh is. It's going to end up just being liquid mess. It's against that, in a sense, that the project of retaining the voice is so attractive.

The last text that I'm going to treat as a coda is, in some ways, the most famous text, "The Fall of the House of Usher." People have read this story about the protagonist who visits his friend, Roderick Usher, in this decaying mansion. They've seen this as an allegory in some ways of the South, the kind of picture of decay, a picture of rot, a decaying culture, perhaps. I don't know if Poe ever meant it that way. If you see it that way, you can see that it leads to eventually,

Absolom, Absolom! of Faulkner, a critique of a whole antebellum culture.

He goes to this house because his friend, Usher, has called for help. People have said, "Well even that is connected." That here, too, maybe we have the parts of the psyche that Usher and the narrator are in some sense figurative or symbolic brothers, and one needs the help of the other. When you get there, it gets triangulated because when he comes to the house, he realizes that there's also the sister, Madeline, who is dying, and she too is a twin, so that she's connected to Usher. You get this sense that all of this is an allegory of the fissured soul again, of all of these three figures somehow needing to be together. She dies in the story, and that's it. The death of a beautiful woman—what else? That's what happens in every Poe story. She dies in this story, and in some odd way, this somehow invigorates Usher. He becomes high-spirited, even though he's a little bit manic. He has been writing dirges, he paints tombs, and he reads the *Office of the Dead*. He becomes energized. That strikes me again as absolutely right for Poe, that dying empowers. Dying feeds. Dying is a blood transfusion.

In fact, Poe's work is to be understood as a kind of necrophilia. We are all living on the blood of the dead. That's what sustains us. We think that it just goes through our own system. In fact, we are feeding on others. You could take it as a view of memory. It's when the dead aren't quite dead. If they're really dead, they're gone from you. But insofar as the dead live in us, as we remember them, as we love them, as we hate them, then you could say that that's a way of understanding their blood continually being in you. I'm speaking figuratively, but Poe, of course, is literal. He's going to show you these things in a new kind of insulate, graphic form. The theme song of this story is "She wasn't dead when we buried her. We put her living into the tomb." It's repeated several times in the story. Again, it just underscores my point. Of course she's not quite dead. As dead, she's not interesting. It's as dying that she's performing the work that is necessary.

This is our return to this model of a kind of psychic civil war that we saw in "William Wilson," but there's nothing static about it. It's a series, a dynamic of sorts. To murder one's beloved or one's double is a kind of central formula in Poe for making art. It's the creative process. It's the way to free yourself—to empower yourself. Yet, you don't want to be free in the sense of getting clear of all of this because that's your material. You're writing about exactly those things. This is the internal wiring of the psyche, as Poe understands it. This is the way in which life is financed. We live on the flow of blood from those that we love. Love, in itself, is inseparable here from a kind of feeding on, and, of course in Poe's case, it comes into a kind of murder so that this story can be read as allegoric, not just of the South, but also of the very complex set of transactions, of appropriations, of transfusions that characterize our intercourse with the people that we most love and who, in fact, we also are.

Lecture Twelve
Poe's Legacy—The Self as "Haunted Palace"

Scope:

Is Poe just horrific and sensational? Or are there other reasons why we return to him, why we cannot quite forget him? A look at several of Poe's briefest and most achieved short stories, "The Black Cat," "The Tell-Tale Heart" and "The Pit and the Pendulum," will show just how rich and bristling the Poe territory is. "The Black Cat" comments, as Poe writes, "on mere household events," and in it we can see a gruesome parable about the sexuality and violence that subtend Poe's horror stories and appear in shockingly displaced form. "The Tell-Tale Heart" is Poe's masterpiece about murder as an Oedipal event of liberation, and we will see that the project of putting out the "Old Man's" eye is a phantasm of cultural as well as psychotic dimensions. To bring this to language constitutes Poe's signature. As for "The Pit and the Pendulum," it remains Poe's most gruesome and perfectly constructed form of torture; we shall see that it is also an emblem of life caught in time and space.

Objectives: Upon completion of this lecture, you should be able to:

1. Explain the role Poe allocates to repression in "The Black Cat."

2. Summarize the narrative paradox at the center of "The Tell-Tale Heart."

3. Summarize why Poe can well be considered a "master builder" of fiction.

Outline

I. "The Black Cat" is one of Poe's most suggesting and shocking pieces; it seems to pick up primitive notions of dismemberment and violation, but to keep muted its most far-reaching violence.

   A. Poe's opening lines are interesting. This story is called both "wild" and "homely;" its plot is referred to as mere "household events." We are warned that this is more than a pet story.

      1. If we are prepared to play with Poe's language, then "wild"="willed," and that equation touches on the manic assertiveness at the core of these events.

2. In the same vein, "homely"=space/spouse, and we can begin to see in these events a reconfiguration of married life.

B. Poe's cheerful domestic group—man, wife, and pet—breaks radically with most sentimental arrangements, turning them into horror; yet we shall see that sentiment is there nonetheless.

1. Poe's subject here allows him an unaccustomed tenderness and feeling, in the narrator's affections for home life.

2. We begin to see something awry in the initial reference to cats and witches, and this "Halloween-like" dimension of the story is going to take over.

C. Poe presents as cause for the horrors and violence of this piece "the Fiend Intemperance," or alcoholic excesses. Knowing Poe's history, we can credit this explanation, yet we wonder whether other, still darker motives are in play.

1. The treatment of the cat is at once familiar and suggestive, and references to biting and caressing begin to acquire a faint erotic overtone, causing us to wonder if the "cat story" perhaps represents other stories.

2. Poe's violent move of putting out the cat's eye is not only shocking but touches a primitive chord in us, with intimations of ritual maiming and disfiguring, as well as radical penetration.

3. Poe alludes here to a spirit of "perverseness," an apparently illogical desire to go against both morality and one's own interests. This notion harks back to Poe's view of "The Imp of the Perverse," his classic statement about conflicting and dark inner motives.

4. As violence and misdeed mount, the house burns down, in a kind of symbolic "overloading" of the system. Yet graphic signs of accusation now appear, as if "writing" and "utterance" had a life of their own and could not be quelled even by fire and extinction.

D. At this point, Poe's story becomes a hall of mirrors as cat #2 enters; this patent repetition throws all realism to the winds and calls attention to the hallucinatory and phantasmal dimensions of the piece.

1. As we read about the described cat, we should start thinking about its "double," not so much the first cat as the obscured wife. Notations such as the cat's "covering me with its loathsome caresses" buttress this inference.

2. Over-determined signs begin to mount: we move from the initial picture of hanged cat to a representation of the gallows themselves.

3. The second act of violence by ax actualizes the story's ultimate libidinal project: the wife is murdered. Has the story been about her all along?

4. The narrator then indulges in Poe's recurring and gratifying activity of disposing of bodies, building walls, concealing the crime. We must see in these moves something of the constituent forces of art.

5. Poe's work writes large the Freudian notion of the return of the repressed. The perfectly committed and concealed crime flaunts its "life" over and over, demands to be spoken and insists on coming "out" again. This gives new meaning to "the death of a beautiful woman," for we see it played out again and again.

E. Reflecting on the strange displacements enacted in Poe's tale, we are obliged to reconstruct a kind of erotic map.

1. Two of Poe's tales, "Ligeia" and "Berenice," hover around the compulsive and hypnotic power of eyes and teeth, and we see scenarios that smack of necrophilia and corpse-plunder, a seeking to reach "satisfaction" with these organs.

2. "Returning to the womb" is a familiar concept in that it suggests a desire for innocence and protection. In Poe's stories, this trajectory is enacted in a grisly, displaced fashion, standing in for—fearful—sexual congress itself, and we see mythic clues, such as the "vagina dentata" along the way.

II. "The Tell-Tale Heart" is arguably Poe's most impressive achievement in horror because it seems to play out all of his strengths at once: breathless narrative voice, murder, concealment, and utterance. Moreover, it has symbolic reaches that reward our plumbing them.

A. The double-edged narrative voice that opens this piece is unforgettable, claiming its sanity and broadcasting its madness in the same words.

   1. This artistic economy, by which words function doubly, typifies Poe's work at its best.

   2. Motiveless malignity for the crime appears to be at work here; yet, once again, the reader may not agree with this assessment.

B. The "old man" who is to be the victim of the narrator's plot calls out to us for interpretation.

   1. Is he Father? God? One-eyed Odin? All of these appellations suggest that he is an "authority figure" who must be done in.

   2. The old man is characterized by—and will be struck in—the evil eye. Why does Poe insist on the eye? We sense that censorship, consciousness, and guilt are all at issue here, and that putting out the eye would deliver the narrator from such surveillance.

   3. Poe's tale asks the fundamental question for conscious creatures: How to be free? His answer is not to everyone's taste.

   4. Poe's tale of murdering the "old man," the "king," is maniacal in its repetitions, suggesting a kind of ritual parricide/regicide.

   5. "Out, out, damned spot," the famous Shakespearean line of Lady Macbeth about the impossibility of removing guilt/consciousness, is referenced in this piece.

C. The beating heart both begins and ends this hypnotic tale. Why?

   1. Whose? is the first question we ask—the victim's or the narrator's? Is there a difference?

   2. The beating heart is also the very heartbeat of narrative, the verbal lifeline that pumps energy from one self to another, from writer to reader.

   3. Poe once again suggests that the psyche has only one recurrent tale: murder. Yet, as always, murder is a continuous affair, a "living" proposition in Poe.

   4. "Buried alive," central here as in so many pieces, is the condition of memory, guilt, and consciousness.

5. Poe can be seen as the man in whom nothing dies, in whom all is put to death and brought to life relentlessly, ritualistically.

III. "The Pit and the Pendulum."

    A. One of Poe's most famous tales, this piece constructs an elaborate torture situation, historically situated, and goes on to leave this image in our mind as the very epitome of human life.

    B. If we consider the details of Poe's setting—a blade that descends over time, a pit that opens into space—we realize the philosophical dimensions of Poe's construct.

IV. Poe's artistic life resembles his stories. We think he is buried and gone, but he is shown to be alive and well.

    A. Whitman's final tribute is expressed as a dream/vision that looks, to the entire world, like a Poe-text.

    B. Hart Crane, who knew something about being a "cursed" poet, experienced a "twinship" with Poe.

    C. Poe must be seen as the master builder of the haunted house, the man who presides over a kingdom of living death, of murder as a form of life, which we gradually come to see as a figure of the way we live.

        1. Poe, then, is the great, uncensored seer, "diving into the wreck" of psyche.

        2. Poe is not just a visionary; he is also the seeker of knowledge who is aware that "knowing" kills. And thus his stories ask: how to know, in art, and yet keep alive?

Readings:

Essential: Poe, "The Raven," "Eldorado," "Annabel Lee," "The Philosophy of Composition," "William Wilson," "The Cask of Amontillado," "The Facts in the Case of M. Valdemar," "The Fall of the House of Usher," "The Black Cat," "The Tell-Tale Heart" in *Poetry and Tales* (Library of America, 1984)

Recommended: Lawrence, *Studies in Classic American Literature* (Viking, 1964); Levin, *The Power of Blackness* (Vintage, 1958); Hoffman, *Poe Poe Poe Poe Poe Poe* (Doubleday, 1972)

Topics for Further Consideration:

1. Discuss the implications of "the poet as maker" vs. "the poet as seer." Summarize which vision of artistic creation you subscribe to.

2. Poe is accused of being shamelessly sensationalist and superficial; defend the case that he provides us with a meaningful representation of human feeling.

Lecture Twelve—Transcript
Poe's Legacy—The Self as "Haunted Palace"

This is Lecture Twelve, and it's the third and final lecture on Edgar Allan Poe. In it, I would like to concentrate most on two of Poe's shortest and pithiest and perhaps most primitive pieces that have a kind of violence, and that really seems to touch on a kind of chord that we don't know how to interpret. There's a kind of need here for dismembering—for ritual destruction—that we need to ponder. Then I'll close with some brief remarks on the "Pit and the Pendulum," which is one of his most famous stories. The two short ones that I'm going to work with more are "The Black Cat" and "The Tell-Tale Heart," and then we'll try to close up shop on Poe if we can—although I'd like to keep him haunting, nonetheless.

As I indicated in my last lecture, something about the dynamics of these stories is what I think is most engaging. He seems at once so melodramatic and so horrific. His work seems to be clothed in the conventions of the gothic; yet one senses that, at every turn, he is exposing—at least what he takes to be, or what he experiences in himself as—internal wiring, as the actual negotiations of the psyche. The things that are happening in his stories are happening always in drag; they're in disguise by displacement. Something else is being told in these stories. It's as if the kind of grotesque and extravagant language and plots that he invents, were there to get into the open something that is otherwise either unavoidable or that just can't be told in any other fashion. There's a kind of crucial work being done in his stories, is really what I want to say. There's nothing gratuitous about Poe's text. Perhaps we will be willing to credit him with more seriousness if we can get a handle on that.

"The Black Cat" is really a great Halloween story. It's in some ways, the most awful thing I think that Poe wrote. It has certain scenes that are very hard to read. He describes it, in his first words, as a domestic story. "For the most wild, yet homely narrative, which I am about to pen, I neither expect nor solicit belief." And then he says a few lines later that, "This is a series of mere household events." "Wild," you know—if you're willing to toy with it verbally—seems like "willed." This is a mad story about the will, about the purview of individual volition and how far it could go. He calls it homely, and it is a domestic story, but to my mind it's domestic in the same way that Shakespeare called *Othello* domestic. It's no less tragic and it's no less grand than *Hamlet* and *Lear*. In fact, there are references to *Lear* in this piece. So, yes it is domestic. Maybe all of Poe's work is domestic––I mean in other words, I said "in drag" and in disguise— but the horrible things he's talking about invariably seem to me to refer back to the events of his life, to his love life, and also to his life as a child who was damaged by the death of women "mother figures" that he loved.

In a sense, he's been domestic from beginning to end. This is a story, however, that brings in the domestic in a rather unusual way in Poe. This is a story that gives us a certain amount of "affective effusion." This character speaks in ways that Poe's characters usually don't.

> …I was noted for the docility and humanity of my disposition. My tenderness of heart was even so conspicuous as to make me the jest of my companions. I was especially fond of animals, and was indulged by my parents with a great variety of pets. With these I spent most of my time, and never was so happy as when feeding and caressing them.

I want you to think about this whole cluster of gestures and motifs. There is a kind of intimacy here—feeding, caressing. Caressing is a word, you know, that doesn't just extend to pets. I mean one thinks of that as a gesture that also links loving people. I think the story is equally about that. There, therefore, is a kind of tenderness, there's a kind of warmth in this story that is unusual for Poe. Yet we note how mercurial it is. This same predisposition towards tenderness, closeness, intimacy, can instantly become hatred, violence, and murder, which of course is what's going to happen in the piece. It's as if once you move into that realm, one becomes the other. Now this is not a new concept. But in this story, it seems to me, Poe is really going to work it very far. Of course, the great object of this is going to be the cat, Pluto. They have a lot of animals. They had had birds, goldfish, dog, rabbits, monkey, but the cat of course is the one that counts, a very beautiful cat.

Then, as if there were no reason for saying it, he says that his wife had made allusion to the ancient popular notion that regarded all black cats as witches in disguise. So there's the Halloween part of the story, if you want; that black cats are witches in disguise. Yet I think it also legitimizes any efforts we're going to make to say that what happens to the cat is probably, in some veiled way, a reflection of how he feels about witches and wives. The connection between women and cats is going to be pretty central here.

We are told by the story—and I think it's an absolute cover, even though it has its truth—that the protagonist does the horrendous things he does, which are going to entail dismembering and murder, because of the "themed intemperance." That's Poe's term for alcohol. He drinks too much. Well, knowing Poe, that has its credibility. Yet it seems to me unmistakably the case that, that is a façade; and that what is really happening has a deeper, more insidious kind of logic than alcohol, which after all, can be a kind of cover, alibi, and an excuse. "Well, I was drunk. That's why I did that." I think that the story doesn't really take it very seriously. We do know that when he was drunk, he even offered his wife personal violence. Again, he said, "Well, it wasn't me, it was the drink in me that did it." We've learned, not only for moral reasons to not allow that kind of explanation, but also to suspect it as bad faith in the first place—violence that comes out as violence that has often been brewing anyway. Certainly that's the case with this story. Again, it's that same duality: tenderness, violence. These are the twins again. This is the two William Wilson's—or this is Jekyll-Hyde? The loving person becomes the killing person very quickly in Poe.

The cat is going to be the site for all of this conflict—for all of this to get played out. As I said, I think it's a kind of displaced site because other things are happening. He loves to caress this cat, and yet when he is drunk, things get out of control.

> One night, returning home much intoxicated, from one of my haunts about town, I fancied that the cat avoided my presence. I seized him; when, in his fright at my violence, he inflicted a slight wound upon my hand with his teeth. The fury of a demon instantly possessed me. I knew myself no longer. My original soul seemed, at once, to take its flight from my body and a more than fiendish malevolence, gin-nurtured, thrilled every fiber of my frame. I took from my waistcoat a pen-knife, opened it, grasped the poor beast by the throat, and deliberately cut one of its eyes from the socket!

As I said, this is the primitive story. This is the story that really reaches back to a kind of ritual dismembering and maiming. It's also the case, as you probably know, that in Freudian terms to blind someone is always symbolic of castration. That's how Freud reads the edifice. That's how that story closes is the edifice, which has seen his eyes, have been the agents of the organs of transgression and, therefore, he puts them out. I think that this story will support that reading as well, that there is a kind of terrible violence here that moves into a primitive stratum that we're really hard put to know how to characterize. There's a kind of hatred here, an almost spastic sense of revenge and control, a volitional act by the body that "this cat could do that to me. I can do something so much worse."

You also have to see it as this is the same animal that he has caressed. This is how far the spectrum goes. Again, it's a domestic story. It's a home story. Caressing the cat, the cat scratching me. You've got to be willing to toy with the idea that there's an erotic connection to all of this. Maybe if he's talking about love life, I'm challenging the view that Edgar Allan Poe lived platonically with his child bride. I'm suggesting that, in the relationship between this man and this cat, that moves from caressing, biting on the one hand, biting can be love play of sorts. It's not really an effort for this cat to wound him and then, all of a sudden, to an explosion of violence with maiming and murders—all of that needs to be considered in its widest possible dimensions.

Poe ascribes a lot of that to one of his own pet theories, which is perverseness. He's written a piece that's very well known called the "Imp of the Perverse" In it, perverseness is really the proclivity that we have to do things against our self-interest, to do things that we don't want to do. Freud would have had no trouble understanding this assertion, that this is what id is all about is that it couldn't care less what ego or superego have in mind. Appetite works against other kinds of interests of ours, because it has its own hunger and need at stake. I think Poe understands all of that. He doesn't use the same language Freud would, but he understands that we frequently do things that are dreadful, and all he can really say is that we do them because they're dreadful. But he doesn't say it's because we're evil. What he's really trying to get at more clinically is that there's something in us that is more powerful than any of the kind of governing restrictions of the social or moral life, and that at key moments we will obey those needs. So that's how he accounts for what happens in the story. We will want to go beyond such a notion this perverse and unpack that as to what might really be going on here.

Needless to say that putting out the cat's eye is just one stage. I mean after all, once you're on a roll you've got to go further than that. "So one morning in cold blood I slipped a noose around its neck." This is predominantly because this cat had continued to be affectionate to him. He can't stand that. "I slipped a noose about its neck and hung it to the limb of a tree, hung it with the tears streaming from my eyes." Now you've got the two Poe's here, or the two Wilson's or whatever. "Tears streaming from my eyes, and with the bitterest remorse in my heart, hung it because I knew it had loved me." And that's a good statement. "And because I felt it had given me no reason of offense, hung it because I knew that in so doing I was committing a sin, a deadly sin."

It all comes together here, that he can't bear being loved. Again I want you to think about Poe's home arrangements. Love is terrifying. I think it somehow exposes a kind of vulnerability that is just intolerable. That may be one reason that it excites this kind of violent response, which is murder or damage. Now, because this is Poe, of course, this is just the beginning. I mean you can't go much worse than hanging a cat, but the story can go further. What's great about Poe is nothing ever remains secret. He's the opposite of Hawthorne in that regard. Hawthorne's work just revolves around trying to ferret out the secrets or to speculate and conjecture what they are. In Poe's work, the secrets always come out. I mean it's as if censorship is the funniest game in town because it will always collapse, so that they come out—but they get rewritten—and he's splendidly graphic. So in this case, all of a sudden he sees on a plaster wall in a *bas relief* upon the surface of a wall—this is after his house is burned down, which is a kind of obvious, very heavy-handed symbolic punishment for killing the cat—on the one wall that's left in the house, the figure of a gigantic cat.

"The impression was given with an accuracy truly marvelous. There was a rope about the animal's neck." You do something and you hope that you can get it hidden, and sure enough. This is real nightmare logic. All the things—all the garbage of your life in a nightmare—just comes pouring onto the scene, and the one person that you can never hide from is yourself. I think that's what happens, gets played out over and over in this piece. Well again, this piece is really almost surreal, because—would you believe—cat #2 comes onto the scene. Now, you know, repetition device. Here's the rhyme. Cat #1 followed by cat #2. Looks the same way. Even has an eye out. One difference only; it has a little mark of white hair which is going to become a nice little graphic moment for this white hair to also project a message.

This cat repeated the same scenario. This cat has a great fondness for the speaker. "Its evident fondness for myself rather disgusted and annoyed." He really can't deal with fondness. "And so this cat covered me. Whenever I sat it would crouch beneath my chair or spring upon my knees covering me with its loathsome caresses. If I rose to walk, it would get between my feet and nearly throw me down, or fastening its long and sharp claws in my dress clamber in this manner to my breast." This is a kind of suffocating intimacy. Again, I want you to think erotically, that this is a weird in-drag version perhaps of lovemaking or lying in bed with another person. It's a kind of intolerable closeness. Well of course you must know what's going to happen. Cat #2 is going to go in the same way.

He has decided to murder this cat. He can't bear it. He's got to get rid of this terrible curse. Here's how he does it.

> The cat followed me down our steep stairs, and, nearly throwing me headlong, exasperated me to madness. Uplifting an axe, and forgetting, in my wrath, the childish dread which it had hitherto stayed my hand, I aimed a blow at the animal which, of course, would have proved instantly fatal had it descended as I wished.

He doesn't quite get to the animal. Why not? Ah! "But the blow was arrested by the hand of my wife. Goaded, by the interference, into a rage more than the demoniacal, I withdrew my arm from her grasp and buried the axe in her brain." Finally, the story has dropped the other shoe. I think it's been about the wife all along. Now she has the axe in her brain. "She fell dead on the spot, without a groan." There's not a word of remorse. There's almost not a word further about the wife. It's like he's gotten it out of his system. The cat has effectively served as the cover, the drag, for all the things that he wants to say in the first place. Then you have the customary Poe activity of a very enjoyable act of burying the body, cutting it up in pieces if you need to, figuring out the various ways that you're going to dispose of it. This is enormously appealing to Poe. This is part of the work of art it seems to me—brickwork and the whole thing. Of course, it won't succeed, just like the others never do. The graphic impulse at heart in his work is that this thing would get broadcast, as it does. He will invite the police in and will be preening and parading about his perfectly concealed crime, and needless to say, it will all come amok, because there will be the exposure; that the corpse will show through. It always does.

It happens here too. Finally, he's swooning. He keeps hearing this thing—he hears the sob of a child—and sure enough it all comes about. They're tearing at the wall, the police, "and the corpse already greatly decayed and plotted with gore, stood erect before the eyes of the spectators. Upon its head with red extended mouth and solitary eye of fire sat the hideous beast, the cat." Wife and cat bonded together, the team that he's tried to do in. He has done them in, but he hasn't done them in, because they are always there. They can't be. They can be killed, but they can't be gotten rid of. Moreover, they can't disappear because they are the lifeblood of the story, if you will. They continue to assert their authority in his mind. Also that's the graphic imperative in Poe that it will ultimately right itself out. That's what happens here.

That's one of his most grizzly stories because most of us, when we read about dismembering, it just simply is hard for us to handle it—and gouging out eyes. I had intended to allude, and I'll just say a word to two stories, "Ligeia" and "Berenice," because they are also about displacements in Poe. "Ligeia" is a story of a woman who comes back from the dead, and it's that same kind of graphic imperative. She's the first wife who's been replaced by the second, but replacement never works in Poe, just like censorship doesn't. All of a sudden this woman—we have put her living into the tomb, as we hear in the "House of Usher"—is not dead. She is there. She reappears. You can never stop things in Poe. In Ligeia, there is a loved woman who, in this case, has these mesmerizing teeth. Then, in a scene that we never really get told, it seems that when she dies the husband has gone down and taken out all of her teeth. There they are at the end of the story. The teeth are on display.

There's an obsession with orifices. I want you to think of that to as displaced sexuality of sorts, with teeth. I want to suggest that the Poe stories are frequently about returning to the womb. I want you to think of it in the most graphic sense of returning to the womb. Not as a return to innocence and protection, the way we think of people returning to their childhood, but I want you to think of it in terms of his own relationship, his sexual relationship with a woman, and the teeth therefore are the "vagina dentata," the teethed womb that is a sexual nightmare for the male who's terrified of what it could mean to think literally about moving into the womb. I think some of that is part of the terror that's in this work.

The story that I'd like to focus on is "The Tell-Tale Heart," which I think is every bit as fine as "The Black Cat." It's about a murder, but it's a murder that really starts to resonate. It opens in classic Poe fashion about a man telling us over and over how clever and sane he is, and the more he says it and the more breathless he is, the more obvious it is to us that he's not sane at all, that his very declarations of sanity brand him mad. His job in the story is to tell us how he killed an old man. As is frequently the case in Poe, he says, there was no reason to do it. "A love passion there was none, object there was none. I loved the old man. He'd never wronged me. He had never given me insult. For his gold I had no desire. I think it was his eye." Back to eyes—got to get the old man's eye.

Much of the most interesting work in the story has to do with focusing on that eye. The raise of a lantern illuminates the eye. Kill the old man's eye. Put out his eye. Well, you know, that's really symbolic stuff. As I said, blinding is, in Freud's theme, castration. For putting out the old man's eye and killing the old man, "No motive," says the protagonist. "I loved him." Okay fine. You loved him. Killing the old man is something from Sophocles, Oedipus, on about slaying the king, slaying the father, about doing in that authority in order to emancipate one's self. If you focus it on the eye—leave aside castration now—it's like you can't bear being seen by the authority of the father, the authority of the old man, seen wise —again, childhood fears—seen masturbating, and seen doing things that you don't want to be seen doing. It's as simple as that. Putting out the eye again, for my money, seems to hum in this story.

This father is like a god figure. He's like one-eyed Odin. He's the evil eye, as is something important in a lot of mythological sense systems. He spies on the speaker. He is consciousness itself. He's a projection of seeing one's self. Put out the eye. Get clear at last. Murdering the king, and I want to suggest that one reference to murdering the king here is, in fact, Shakespearean, because when he finally does it, or when he's about to do it, he's got the lantern reflected on the eye. This eye was wide open. "I could see nothing else of the old man's face or person, for I had directed the ray as if by instinct precisely upon the damned spot." And of course if you know your Shakespeare and you know *Macbeth*, "Out, out damned spot," that's a story too about killing the king. Poe has packed this with references to destroying authority, to destroying kingship. "I had no motive," he says. Well this story is crawling with motives.

Once again, doing in the king is always easier said than done. You can do it, but you can't get rid of the king. The story, in some of its most wonderful passages, once again moves into that graphic mode where what is done, comes back—and Freud might call it the return of the repressed. I think it's more than that. There's an "artistic imperative". I call it the "graphic imperative." The beating heart is one. It's just like a tattoo. "The hellish tattoo of the heart increased. It grew quicker and quicker and louder and louder." This is before he kills the old man. That's when he does it. Then he kills him three ways. He puts out his eye, suffocates him, and he dismembers him. He really wants to get the job done. He invites in the police. He's properly concealed that same sense of great pleasure and pride. "I've done the job well." Got him definitely concealed, invites the police, but the heart keeps beating. The heart keeps beating. He hears it. It gets louder and louder and louder.

I want to suggest to you something about that heartbeat. In my last lecture I said that there's a kind of blood system that works in Poe, and I called it necrophilia, that the living are in some sense circulating and absorbing the blood of the dead. Here I want to say that it's even more mobile and more insistent and turbulent than that. It's not just flowing blood, it's the beating heart. It's the beating heart. I'd like to suggest that's the beating heart of literature, of narrative, that makes things live over time. It's the same story of "Valdemar," of how you could keep the voice beyond the decay of the body. In this case, this beating heart, in a sense, is the life of the loved one. He loved this old man, he said. He's put him away, and yet he continues to live. It's like a mummy of sorts that continues to have its own heartbeat. Of course we can't miss the fact that the beating heart that's been heard is always the beating heart of the speaker. It's the narrator himself. It's his heart that really is the systolic and diastolic of the text.

There's something really quite splendid about the way in which all of this comes full circle in Poe. All of it has to be said. The concealment is always a kind of failed project in Poe—the pleasure, though it gives—and everything that's inside moves outside. It's what Poe's work is. Things that we would like to keep inside, horrible views of our own negotiations and dynamics and worrying, come out in Poe's work. They become art. They become script. They become language. They become sounds that people can interpret, a beating heart that someone can interpret. This is his formula.

The text that I'll just briefly allude to is "The Pit and the Pendulum," which is one of his most famous stories. There are just two things I'll say about it. One is that it's one of the emblematic stories that stick in our minds, because it says that life is incarceration. We know enough about political history, and this story is situated during the days of the Spanish Inquisition, not the Spanish Inquisition. It's a later inquisition, but it's inquisition. We know enough, particularly in our own time since Poe, to know how many people have lived tortured in prison. That's what the story's about. Instead, it's universalized as a kind of image of human life. We're born and die, in prisons.

This prison is a very special prison. It's a particular torture chamber and, you may remember, it consists of a blade that descends over time, and it gets closer. He's tied down, and the blade is going to finally go through his heart. And, it consists of a pit that is opening up—where the walls are going to force him into the pit. I think others have said this—this isn't my invention—this is a brilliant rendition of time and space. That over time this is the sword that descends on all lives. That over time it's like a moving Damocles' sword. It gets closer and closer and finally it cuts you, and finally it destroys you. Of course, the pit would be in a sense, not just the grave, but it's the human subject, the human body in a sense, lost in time and space. That's the prison he's talking about. Both time and space both contain us—and doom us—and that we have no home there. We're in prison. That's just a couple of comments about that.

I want to be able to close by trying to return to Poe's work in a larger sense. I read you the passage from Walt Whitman at the public reburial of Poe's remains, the dedication in 1875. But Whitman wrote a little bit more than that too. He also said this:

> In a dream I once had, I saw a vessel on the sea, at midnight, in a storm. It was no great full-rigg'd ship, nor majestic steamer, steering firmly through the gale, but seem'd one of those superb little schooner yachts I had often seen lying

anchor'd, rocking so jauntily, in the waters around New York, or up Long Island sound—now flying uncontroll'd with torn sails and broken spars through the wild sleet [and winds] and waves of the night. On the deck was a slender, slight, beautiful figure, a dim man, apparently enjoying all the terror, the murk, and the dislocation of which he was the centre and the victim. That figure of my lurid dream might stand for Edgar Poe, his spirit, his fortunes, and his poems—themselves all lurid dreams.

What's beautiful there is that Whitman becomes Poe. That's a dream state that Poe could have written. That's not typical Whitman at all. I said this man is the most influential man in some ways in American literature, and I was alluding to his impact on the French side of things. That then returns. Whitman, in trying to do his own homage to Poe, is infected by Poe, and gives us a Poe nightmarish landscape of being adrift in a storm and enjoying the terror of which you are both the center and the victim.

A last reference, which I think is quite haunting: This is the great poem by Hart Crane called "The Bridge." In this poem, Crane, who was as much I think a cursed man as Poe was, writes this passage, which is the segment of this very difficult form, where he's in the subway, and he goes under the river. The subway goes deeper and deeper under. It's like Dante and his *Inferno*. He begins to have visions of people in the subway car.

> Whose head is swinging from the swollen strap?
>
> Whose body smokes along the bitten rails,
>
> Bursts from a smoldering bundle far behind
>
> In the back forks of the chasms of the brain,—
>
> Puffs from a riven stump far out behind
>
> In interborough fissures of the mind…?

There is a wonderful sense in which the subway track—going under the river—all of this becomes a figure for the structure of the brain, for the patterns of thought. This is so Poe-like.

> And why do I often meet your visage here,
>
> Your eyes like agate lanterns—on and on

Below the toothpaste and the dandruff ads?

—And did their riding eyes right through your side,

And did their eyes like unwashed plasters ride?

And Death, aloft,—gigantically down

Probing through you—toward me, O evermore!

I mean, he's reciting half of Poe here.

And when they dragged your retching flesh,

Your trembling hands that night through Baltimore—

That last night on the ballot rounds, did you,

Shaking, did you deny the ticket, Poe?

It's a perfect, I think, homage and recognition of this man, who is the great builder of the haunted house, and the great occupant of the haunted house, and I think the great visionary who gives it to us, so that we, for a moment, could live in it too.

Comprehensive Bibliography

Barbour, Brian M., ed. *Benjamin Franklin: Critical Views.* Englewood Cliffs, NJ: Prentice-Hall, 1979.

Bercovitch, Sacvan. *The Office of the Scarlet Letter.* Baltimore, MD: John Hopkins University Press, 1991.

Bloom, Harold. *Modern Critical Interpretations: Death of a Salesman.* New York: Chelsea House, 1988.

―――. *Modern Critical Interpretations: Moby-Dick.* New York: Chelsea House.

―――. *The Western Canon.* New York: Riverhead, 1994.

―――. *William Faulkner's* Absalom, Absalom! New York: Chelsea House, 1987.

―――. *William Faulkner's* The Sound and the Fury. Philadelphia, PA: Chelsea House, 1998.

Bradbury, Malcolm. *The Modern American Novel.* New York: Oxford University Press, 1984.

Cox, C. B., and Arnold Hinchliffe, eds. *The Waste Land: A Collection of Critical Essays.* London: MacMillan, 1968.

Cox, James M. *Robert Frost: A Collection of Critical Essays.* Englewood Cliffs, NJ: Prentice-Hall, 1962.

Crane, Stephen. *Prose and Poetry.* New York: Library of America, 1984.

―――. *The Red Badge of Courage.* New York: Norton Critical Edition, 1962.

Dickinson, Emily. *Final Harvest: Emily Dickinson's Poems.* Boston: Little Brown, 1961.

Eliot, T. S. *The Complete Poems and Plays.* New York: Harcourt, Brace & World, 1952.

―――. "Tradition and the Individual Talent." In *Visions and Revisions in Modern American Literary Criticism,* edited by Bernard Oldsley and Arthur Lewis. New York: Dutton, 1962.

―――. "*Ulysses*: Order and Myth." In *Forms of Modern Fiction,* edited by William Van O'Connor. Bloomington, IN: Indiana University Press, 1948.

Elliot, Emery, ed. *The Columbia History of the American Novel.* New York: Columbia University Press, 1991.

Ellison, Ralph. *Invisible Man*. New York: Vintage, 1989.

Emerson, Ralph Waldo. *Essays and Lectures*. New York: New American Library, 1983.

Faulkner, William. *Absalom, Absalom!*. New York: Vintage, 1986.

_____. *As I Lay Dying*. New York: Random House, 1991.

_____. *Go Down, Moses*. New York: Random House, 1991.

_____. *Light in August*. New York: Random House, 1991.

———. *The Sound and the Fury*. New York: Vintage, 1986.

Fisher, Philip. *Hard Facts: Setting and Form in the American Novel*. New York: Oxford University Press, 1987.

Fitzgerald, F. S. *The Great Gatsby*. New York: Scribner's, 1960.

_____. *Tender Is the Night*. New York: Simon and Schuster, 1995.

Franklin, Benjamin. *Writings*. New York: Library of America, 1987.

Frost, Robert. *Selected Poems of Robert Frost*. New York: Holt, Rinehart and Winston, 1963.

Gilbert, Sandra, and Susan Gubar. *The Madwoman in the Attic*. New Haven: Yale University Press, 1979.

Gilman, Charlotte Perkins. *The Yellow Wall-Paper*. Thomas Erskine and Connie Richards, eds. New Brunswick, NJ: Rutgers University Press, 1993.

Hawthorne, Nathaniel. *Novels*. New York: Library of America, 1983.

———. *The Scarlet Letter*. New York: Norton Critical Edition, 1978)

———. *Tales and Sketches*. New York: Library of America, 1982.

Hemingway, Ernest. *A Farewell to Arms*. New York: Scribners, 1987.

_____. *The Garden of Eden*. New York: MacMillan, 1987.

———. *Green Hills of Africa*. New York: Scribner's, 1987.

———. *A Moveable Feast*. New York: Scribner's, 1964.

———. *The Sun Also Rises*. New York: Scribner's, 1986.

Hoffman, Daniel. *Poe Poe Poe Poe Poe Poe Poe*. Garden City, NY: Doubleday, 1972.

Irving, Washington. *History, Tales and Sketches*. New York: Library of America, 1983.

James, Henry. *The Ambassadors*. New York: Norton Critical Edition, 1964.

_____. *The Aspern Papers*. New York: Everyman's Library, 1994.

_____. *The Beast in the Jungle and Other Stories*. New York: Dover, 1993.

———. *The Turn of the Screw*. New York: Norton Critical Edition, 1966.

Kaplan, Justin. *Walt Whitman: A Life*. New York: Simon and Schuster, 1980.

Kazin, Alfred. *An American Procession*. New York: Vintage, 1985.

———. *On Native Grounds*. New York: Harcourt, Brace & Co., 1942.

Kenner, Hugh. *A Homemade World: The American Modernist Writers*. New York: William Morrow, 1975.

Lawrence, D. H. *Studies in Classic American Literature*. New York: Viking, 1964.

Lee, A. Robert, ed. *Edgar Allan Poe: The Design of Order*. Totowa, NJ: Barnes and Noble, 1987.

Levin, Harry. *The Power of Blackness: Hawthorne, Poe, Melville*. New York: Vintage, 1958.

Lyne, William. "The Signifying Modernist: Ralph Ellison and the Limits of the Double Consciousness." *PMLA* (March 1992).

Lynn, Kenneth. *Hemingway*. New York: Simon and Schuster, 1987.

Matthieseen, F. O. *The Achievement of T. S. Eliot*. New York: Oxford University Press, 1958.

———. *American Renaissance*. New York: Oxford University Press, 1941.

Melville, Herman. *Billy Budd, Sailor and Other Stories*. New York: Penguin, 1967.

———. *Moby-Dick*. New York: Norton Critical Edition, 1967.

———. *Pierre, Israel Potter, The Confidence Man, Tales and Billy Budd*. New York: Library of America, 1984.

———. *Redburn, White-Jacket, Moby-Dick*. New York: Library of America, 1983.

Miller, Arthur. *The Crucible*. New York: Penguin, 1995.

_____. *Death of a Salesman*. New York: Penguin, 1976.

Moorton, Richard F., ed. *Eugene O'Neill's Century*. New York: Greenwood, 1991.

Morrison, Toni. *Beloved*. New York: New American Library, 1988.

_____. *The Song of Solomon*. New York: NAL-Dutton, 1993.

_____. *Sula*. New York: NAL-Dutton, 1993.

Oberg, Barbara, and Harry Stout, eds. *Benjamin Franklin, Jonathan Edwards and the Representation of American Culture*. New York: Oxford University Press, 1993.

O'Meally, Robert, ed. *New Essays on Invisible Man*. Cambridge: Cambridge University Press, 1988.

O'Neill, Eugene. *Complete Plays: 1932-1943*. New York: Library of America, 1988.

———. *Long Day's Journey Into Night*. New Haven: Yale University Press, 1965.

Paglia, Camille. *Sexual Personae*. New York: Vintage, 1991.

Parker, R.B. *Twentieth Century Interpretations of* The Glass Menagerie. Englewood Cliffs, NJ: Prentice-Hall, 1983.

Poe, Edgar Allan. *Poetry and Tales*. New York: Library of America, 1984.

Poirier, Richard. Robert Frost: *The Work of Knowing*. Stanford, CA: Stanford University Press, 1990.

Porter, David. *Dickinson: The Modern Idiom*. Cambridge, MA: Harvard University Press, 1981.

Reynolds, David. *Beneath the American Renaissance*. Cambridge, MA: Harvard University Press, 1988.

Samuels, Charles. *The Ambiguity of Henry James*. Urbana: University of Illinois Press, 1971.

Steinbeck, John. *The Grapes of Wrath*. New York: Viking, 1958.

Stowe, Harriet Beecher. *Three Novels*. New York: Library of America, 1982.

Thompson, Judith. *Tennessee Williams' Plays: Memory, Myth and Symbol*. New York: Peter Lang, 1987.

Thoreau, Henry David. *A Week on the Concord and Merrimack Rivers, Walden; Or Life in the Woods, The Maine Woods, Cape Cod*. New York: Library of America, 1985.

Tompkins, Jane. "Sentimental Power: *Uncle Tom's Cabin* and the Politics of Literary History." In *The New Feminist Criticism*, edited by Elaine Showalter. New York: Pantheon, 1985.

Twain, Mark [Samuel Langhorne Clemens]. *Adventures of Huckleberry Finn*. New York: Norton Critical Edition, 1977.

_____. *The Adventures of Tom Sawyer*. New York: Penguin, 1986.

———. *Mississippi Writings*. New York: Library of America, 1982.

———. *Pudd'nhead Wilson and Those Extraordinary Twins*. New York: Norton Critical Edition, 1980.

Warren, Robert Penn. *Faulkner: A Collection of Critical Essays*. Englewood Cliffs, NJ: Prentice-Hall, 1966.

Weinstein, Arnold. *The Fiction of Relationship*. Princeton, NJ: Princeton University Press, 1988.

———. *Nobody's Home: Speech, Self and Place in American Fiction from Hawthorne to DeLillo*. New York: Oxford University Press, 1993.

———. *Vision and Response in Modern Fiction*. Ithaca, NY: Cornell University Press, 1974.

Weinstein, Philip M. *Faulkner's Subject: A Cosmos Nobody Owns*. New York: Cambridge University Press, 1992.

———. *What Else But Love? The Ordeal of Race in Faulkner and Toni Morrison*. New York: Columbia University Press, 1997.

Whitman, Walt. *Complete Poetry and Collected Prose*. New York: Library of America, 1982.

Williams, Tennessee. *A Streetcar Named Desire and Other Plays*. London: Penguin, 1962.

Wyatt, David, ed. *New Essays on the Grapes of Wrath*. Cambridge: Cambridge University Press, 1990.

Young, Philip. "Fallen from Time: The Mythic Rip Van Winkle." In *Visions and Revisions in Modern American Literary Criticism*, edited by Bernard Oldsley and Lewis Arthur. New York: Dutton, 1962.